Ellen 1992

TEACHING
FAMILY
THERAPY

GW00645121

TEACHING FAMILY THERAPY

by
Ros Draper
Myrna Gower
and
Clare Huffington

Systemic Thinking and Practice Series
Series Editors:
David Campbell and **Ros Draper**

KARNAC BOOKS
London 1991 New York

First published in 1990 by DC Publishing

This edition published in 1991 by H. Karnac (Books) Ltd.
58 Gloucester Road, London SW7 4QY

Distributed in the U.S.A. by
Brunner/Mazel, Inc
19, Union Square West,
New York, NY 10003

© 1991 Ros Draper, Myrna Gower and Clare Huffington

The rights of Ros Draper, Myrna Gower and Clare Huffington to
be identified as authors of this work have been asserted in
accordance with ss 77 and 78 of the Copyright Design and
Patents Act 1988.

ISBN 1 85575 021 X

All Rights Reserved. No part of this publication may be
reproduced, stored in a retrieval system, or transmitted in any
form or by any means, electronic, mechanical, photocopying,
recording or otherwise, without the prior permission of the
Publisher.

A CIP catalogue record for this book is available from the
British Library.

Printed in Great Britain by BPCC Wheatons Ltd, Exeter

Contents

Foreword

The value of this book cannot be over-estimated. The clear and concise theoretical summaries, interspersed with the often deceptively simple but innovative and creative exercises are invaluable. The stated aim of each exercise, the emphasis on feedback to inform the teacher of the progress of the group, the suggestions for reading and such chapters as "First Aid for Teachers" could all be a lifeline for those who are planning a new course or teaching for the first time.

However, this book is also for the experienced, whose teaching may be in danger of becoming stereotyped. Ways to integrate new epistemologies, holding teaching sessions in the form of a debate, using T.V. "soaps" to enhance systemic thinking and fairy tales as a game to contrast models of therapy are all refreshing new ideas.

Every chapter in this excellent book has direct relevance for teachers of family therapy. For instance on a recent visit to a new training course in Harare, Zimbabwe, the trainers there were struggling with how to teach the integration of different models of therapy. This issue is clearly and deftly dealt with in this book and it made me realise how useful it will be for emerging training establishments.

But perhaps the authors most impressive and helpful contribution is the way they draw on their own experience. They not only describe how to organise and run the groups but they help teachers to anticipate pitfalls and suggest ways to enhance participation.

In the introduction, the authors state that "teaching is a constant process of evolution for us". This is described in their short historical presentation of the courses developed at the Tavistock Clinic, in which they used graduates of the Advanced Course in Family Therapy as teachers. Over the years this leads to the four level teaching hierarchy described.

This evolution gives me great pleasure, as it shows how the process I and others started in the early seventies has developed in the hands of our colleagues. The first edition of this book has already had considerable influence. This second edition will continue to benefit all those who are involved in laying sound foundations for teaching in family therapy.

Rosemary Whiffen
Dorset
1991

Acknowledgements

We would like to thank all our teachers past and present; our teaching colleagues at the Tavistock and elsewhere, the students who have enabled us to develop these ideas and the families who have inspired us to want to teach what we have come to understand about how to manage the complexities of life.

EDITORS' FOREWORD

This is an invaluable book for anyone teaching Family Therapy. It is unique for its extensive teaching exercises which are supported by theoretical discussions and a guide to the practical problems in setting up and carrying out teaching sessions.

Ros Draper, Myrna Gower and Clare Huffington are experienced and respected teachers in the Family Therapy field. They have recently been organising courses and supervising other teachers of Family Therapy courses. Through their collective experience they have produced a book which will be used like a handbook for teachers for years to come.

The theoretical underpinning of the book utilises systemic thinking to describe the creation of a teaching–learning context. This context – which is built upon the feedback from different parts of the teaching 'system' – frames all of the teaching subsequently described in the book.

The authors have also included a section about practical problems, which are seldom written about, yet which can make the difference between a good teaching session and a disaster. They discuss situations such as: *What do you do when the equipment fails?* – which are the bane of every Family Therapy teacher.

The heart of this book is the series of 43 teaching exercises which are grouped according to the different Family Therapy approaches (such as structural, strategic, systemic) which form the structure of the basic Family Therapy course. Each exercise has been carefully designed to create an experience which allows each participant to learn the specific topic being presented. For example, there are exercises to promote the learning of "enactment", "circular questioning" and "reframing". Because the authors have vast experience with these techniques, they are able to describe, for each exercise, the amount of time needed, the level of experience required of participants, and any supplementary reading.

The format of the book is clear and easy-to-read. The book is designed to be a practical aid for teachers, and as such they can open it for reference while teaching – and there are spaces provided for teachers to make their own notes.

There are very few papers or books in the Family Therapy field which describe practical step-by-step teaching techniques. This book clearly fills a gap in the field and will be immensely helpful to teachers.

David Campbell
Ros Draper
London, 1990

Introduction

The thinking presented in this book has developed from the experience of three part-time family therapy courses held at the Tavistock Centre.

The authors have been part of the teaching team of three part-time courses:

A Systems Approach to Families and Organisations Part I
A Systems Approach to Families and Organisations Part II,
Live Supervision in the Work Setting: Part III

Roles in the teaching team include teacher, supervisor and organising tutor. This hierarchy of teachers, supervisors and consultant has led to much discussion and analysis of the issues involved in teaching family therapy. Over time a review of the positions in the system has allowed a better view of the teaching process to develop. Whilst this book is based specifically on the experience gained from these particular courses, our aim is to describe the issues in such a way that the book will be of value to all who are presently involved in teaching family therapy or who are considering setting up courses in family therapy. The material presented includes ideas about course organisation, the process and content (or the what and how) of teaching family therapy to professionals.

The historical context is that, Rosemary Whiffen, an eminent social work practitioner, started the first part-time introductory course in family therapy in the early 1970s. It spanned one academic year consisting of two hours per week for three ten week terms. Initially, a second year was set up for two terms only and each of the two years was regarded as a separate course. Ros Draper began teaching the course in October 1977 and was the third teacher to run the course. The groups in both Part I and Part 11 comprised twelve students, all of whom were social workers.

In October 1979, two additional teachers were recruited to teach the first year and Ros moved to a position of supervising the teaching. This was the first move towards the framework of consultation that is characteristic of the present (1991) approach to our teaching.

The teachers recruited to teach the two courses from October 1979 until October 1987 were all selected from second year trainees or graduates of an Advanced Family Therapy course that was held at the Tavistock Clinic. Teaching was carried out in pairs, as this gave greater opportunity for flexibility, creativity and support. The advanced Family Therapy course (now an MSc in Family Therapy) was the first of its kind in this country and is distinguished by its teaching practice component.

During the years 1979-87 the standard of debate in supervision was high. The teachers were themselves in a training context where the rules dictated the asking of questions and the challenging of ideas. This placed the supervisor in the invaluable position of developing a useful "teaching–learning system" that simultaneously attended to both the training of teachers and the delivery of courses to consumers. What has evolved is a four level hierarchy of course members, teachers, supervisors of teachers and an organising tutor for each course.

The hierarchy concerns accountability and amplifying and maximising the use of feedback. Teachers, supervisors and tutors need to reflect on their teaching in order to be influenced by feedback so that they are able to experience the power of the observer position.

One of our beliefs is that the "teaching–learning system" cannot be connected without the use of feedback. The exercises we present in this book are the ones which we think best take the feedback into account.

Suitable applicants for the course increased and in 1983 the first year intake was expanded to two groups. The quality of teachers was maintained by continuing to recruit from graduates from the Tavistock Clinic advanced courses.

Special attention was paid to the continued requests of course members for a practice component to the course. A third and final course was established in 1985 with the aim of offering mental health professionals regular live supervision in their work settings.

Feedback from the field of family therapy practitioners has shown us that "therapy" is not the way most people describe their work. Health and social services managers tend not to allow the work of their teams to be described in this way for a variety of political and economic reasons. Such work is referred to instead as "case work" or "social work practice", "family work" or "statutory intervention".

We have also found that course members are preoccupied with applying their learning from the course in their own agencies. They often find it more difficult to bring about change in their work systems, if they feel they have to convert people to family therapy rather than if they take back to the agency useful ideas and skills for work with clients.

This kind of feedback has allowed us to emphasise teaching the application of systemic ideas in a variety of contexts and, to give course members the experience of ideas being effective in a variety of agencies. Since the courses became multi-disciplinary in 1984, the work contexts are as diverse as possible.

The thinking in the family therapy community has shifted towards attempts to integrate different models of family therapy and to examine where they are linked and where they diverge from one another. The notion of clearly distinct schools is now being challenged and systems or systemic thinking seems to be considered a heading under which all approaches to family therapy can be subsumed. The field has begun to draw on the work of thinkers and writers, not necessarily family therapists, who are not identified with any particular school, although their ideas may have been brought to attention by workers, of a particular school of family therapy. Some examples are the work of biologists, Maturana and Varela (1980) first brought to our attention by Milan therapists, e.g., Cecchin (1988); philosophical ideas like constructivism in the work of Von Glaserfeld (1984) and Keeney (1988); cybernetics in the work of Von Foerster (1979). There are also ideas from family therapists which have been applied across models; for example, problem-determined systems (Anderson, Goolishian and Windermand, 1987); the reflecting team (Andersen, 1987) and interventive interviewing (Tomm, 1987a, 1987b, 1988).

We do not exclusively teach about family therapy from family therapy models, but also from core systemic ideas, such as the family life cycle, circularity, pattern, roles, myths, beliefs, homoeostasis, contradictions, etc. By developing a systemic orientation to problem solving, course participants are able to evaluate or take an observer position to different family therapy models and gradually identify a personal style of working which is comfortable for them. So, for example, we plan a session on the family life cycle and explore the place this concept has in various family therapy models, seeing for example how central it is in Transgenerational Family Therapy theory and practice. On the other hand, when offering a session on Structural Family Therapy and exploring the core systemic ideas in this model, we might end up looking at the model and the extent to which these ideas are shared by other schools. What, for example, are the similarities and differences between structural interventions and tasks set in Milan Systemic Family Therapy?

Teaching is a constant process of evolution for us. The titles of the courses have changed over the years with developments in the field. Our courses used to be called: *An Introduction to Family Therapy Parts I and II* and *Family Therapy Supervision in the Work Setting Part III*.

They are now (1991) called: *A Systems Approach to Change in Families, Work Groups and Organisations, Parts I and II* and *Systemic Practice in the Work Setting, Part III*.

The changes in course aims are also interesting to observe over time, e.g., in 1980 the aim of *An Introduction to Family Therapy Part I* – was "to provide an opportunity for members to develop the basic skills in family therapy".

In 1989 the same course, called *A Systems Approach to Families and Organisations Part I* aimed "to provide an opportunity for members to learn and develop the basic conceptual and executive skills of a systems approach to families and organisations, and to apply this knowledge in different work contexts". Anti-racist and anti-sexist perspectives have now to be an integral part of the course.

An appreciation of a systems approach as a problem-solving intervention is now well established in the helping professions in this country. Demand for training has increased as has concern about standards. The first AFT Trainers conference was in 1986. This, along with consumer feedback, meant that a more formal evaluation of the teaching was necessary to keep abreast of national standards. In 1988 *Part I* was accredited by The National Association of Family Therapy as an Introductory course. Such accreditation plays an increasingly important part in course evaluation.

This book attempts to raise many issues that can help to clarify the requirements for training teachers in the field. We acknowledge the dilemma of untrained teachers in an area where the expectation has been that any family therapy practitioner has the ability to teach. Effective teaching is a complex task, and teachers of family therapy, like therapists, get "stuck". Using the "stuck" position as feedback in our teaching–learning system has led to an emphasis being placed on carefully planned and creative exercises which can be used by people with different levels of experience. These exercises are intriguingly presented here within the carefully explained teaching context; and, we hope, in a clear and readable form.

We have chosen to concentrate on presenting a variety of teaching exercises because they illustrate our core teaching ideas in action. We have not found a comparable resource for teachers in the family therapy field in this country. Teaching issues are being debated theoretically but there still remains a shortage of practice material which teachers may consult. This book is our attempt to fill this gap.

We intend this book to provide a useful intervention for teachers as a means of consultation to the teaching process and as a contribution to the development of a body of theoretical and practical skills for teachers of family therapy.

Chapter 1

TEACHING SYSTEMIC THINKING

1 THE TEACHING LEARNING SYSTEM

The participants in the teaching–learning system are: organising tutor – supervisor – teacher – course participant. They can be considered as a system when feedback about expectations is communicated between the different subgroups. What is more implicit than explicit at the outset of this process, is that the expectations of all members of the system cannot be met without giving and receiving feedback.

We see the interaction between the people at these different levels as identifying the boundaries of the teaching–learning-system.

The people are:

I   The Supervisor or Course Organising Tutor
II   The Teachers
III The Course Participants
IV   The Agency Context or Course Participants Colleagues

We have chosen certain punctuations or phases in the life of the course to show how the co-evolutionary feedback process facilitates learning.

Phase I

The initial phase includes the negotiations between an institution and the teachers to teach the course. A supervisor and a teacher begin to prepare the course outline and syllabus. When the applicants are offered and accept a place on the course, the teacher/course participants system comes into being.

As both contracts are agreed, i.e., the contract between the institution and the teacher and the contract between the institution and the course applicant, the teaching–learning-system begins.

Phase II

This phase includes the supervisor and teacher developing a shared view about the aims and content of the course. The effect of sharing expectations and fears at this point is to promote enthusiasm and creativity. The supervisor may also offer ideas to the teachers about how to recognise and receive feedback about the learning in the group.

Phase III

At this point, the teachers meet the course members for the first time. They are in a position to explore with the group their expectations and fears about learning on the course. The central focus is to make connections between the course and the agency contexts by encouraging application of learning on the course in course participants' agencies.

Phase IV

Here, course participants begin to feedback to their agencies their learning from the course. This is often a difficult time because the ideas are frequently challenged or rejected by colleagues and participants are put in the position of having to redefine their professional practice.

Phase V

Finally, participants begin to feed-back information about their changing perceptions of themselves and of their agencies within the context of the teaching sessions. They begin to examine with fellow course participants the effects of applying their knowledge and the feedback that it generates. This sometimes leads to aspects of the course being reappraised and changed by teachers.

The loop is completed when a joint meeting occurs between all members of the system, i.e., supervisor, teacher, course participants and agencies. The purpose of these annual meetings is to review everyone's learning.

2 THE FRAMEWORK OF SUPERVISION

It is in the context of regular supervision that teachers can take the course participant's position for a time. Issues discussed range from how to teach a particular concept to how to get a kettle to make coffee for the group. Supervision allows teachers, of whatever therapeutic orientation, to develop an observer position in relation to their teaching. They are then more likely to be able to address feedback from course participants in such a way as to continue responding to the group. A certain amount of dependency develops within the supervision relationship, particularly at the beginning when teachers are unfamiliar with the teaching context and need guidance from the supervisor. The relationship soon evolves to a different level which involves support, sharing of content and process issues and even the exploration of the systemic implications of administrative matters. For example, if one group is unable to use their accustomed room for a particular week, what kind of difference will it make to the groups learning to share a room with another group? How can new members joining the course after a year become integrated into the group?

It is still difficult for teachers to believe that getting stuck is an inevitable part of the process. When the teacher fails to take this feedback into account, it can be confusing and loss of direction can follow. The following dialogue from a supervision session between a teacher who was working jointly with another teacher (who was not present at the session) and the course supervisor (S) illustrates the way supervision helps the teacher (T) develop an observer position:

T: There is a great difference between the groups. Mine doesn't seem to be sophisticated in systemic thinking.

S: How do you know that?

T: Well, the way they ask questions in role plays as therapists and the sort of interventions they gave each other in last weeks agency consultation exercise. They are still giving each other advice!

S: What feedback are you looking for from your group?

T: I would like to be sure that they understand the tasks I asked them to do last time.

S: Is that the same as or different from what the other teacher is looking for?

T: I think the other teacher is looking for how good her group is at systemic thinking and she is pleased with them.

S: Maybe you shouldn't be looking for this feedback from your group. What feedback from the other group is the other teacher not attending to? What struggles are going on in her group? If you drew back a little and observed the meaning of the feedback in your group, would that influence you to have more separate sessions from the other group?

T: Oh, that feels like a relief: I was beginning to feel rather disconnected from my group and tending to see them through the other teacher's eyes. I must negotiate with her to plan the next session so as to allow the groups to be taught separately.

By the application of systemic thinking to the supervision process, the supervisor was challenging the teacher's hypothesis that her group was not doing so well. By suggesting alternative hypotheses or explanations, the possibilities for responding to feedback open to the teacher are maximised and the teacher was no longer confused.

3 DEFINING OUR CONTEXT AS TEACHERS
In order to develop a systemic approach to teaching we begin by defining the context for ourselves as teachers. The key components of becoming a teacher in this context are the invitation to teach, accountability for and supervision of the teaching; relationship with other teachers and resource holders,

e.g., librarian, training department, administration and secretariat.

Teachers' expectations and beliefs about the teaching process lead to questions of other teachers and supervisors like:

> "How will I know if my teaching meets with
> your expectations?"

> "What should I bear in mind from your experience
> last year as I start to teach the same course this year? "

4. DEFINING THE TEACHING CONTEXT FOR COURSE MEMBERS AND THE EFFECT ON SYLLABUS DESIGN

We think that the teaching context becomes clearer for course members when teachers attend to and make explicit their intentions about the following list of teaching issues:

(a) Use of teachers; joint, parallel or separate teaching some or all of the time; degree of integration of teaching groups on the same course, when there are parallel groups attending the same course.

(b) Shifting the context of teaching from individuals, groups, organisations, families often in one exercise; shifting the activity of the group from individual, pairs, small and large group work within the session; use of homework and projects for individuals, pairs and small groups; use of role play, video, discussion tasks and live families.

(c) Theoretical input and approaches to doing this.

(d) Use of exercises.

(e) Use of feedback.

Feedback from course participants is positively encouraged. For instance, we might ask for feedback on how group members conceptualise themselves as a system. This allows us another way in which to provide input or plan exercises around issues like homoeostasis or boundaries. We would anticipate feedback from course members as part of session planning so as to give us manoeuvrability as teachers. Whatever we do, we think about the possible impact on the course participants if the exercise were to be handled in different ways. If, for example, we were to teach two groups together in one group's usual room, how might we address any tendency for the visitors to become passive in relation to the host group? Could we give the visitors very active roles in an exercise involving both groups, e.g., to be a therapy team for a role play family made up from members of the host group?

If one of the teachers were to give some theoretical input to both groups together, to what extent would the group of the non-presenting teacher feel able to embrace these ideas? Would it be important for the other teacher to identify his or her position vis-a-vis the ideas presented in order for the group to move forward? Or would it be sufficient to balance this situation later in the year when the non-presenter can present to both groups?

We think that the implications of the definition of context are often not considered important enough. Even if great efforts are made to anticipate feedback and clearly define contexts, unexpected things still happen; for example, keys are lost, the technician leaves and is not replaced, the teachers do not know when and how much they will be paid. In response to such trials, the teacher learns coping strategies over time through the supervision process.

5. HELPING COURSE PARTICIPANTS TO DEFINE THEIR WORK CONTEXTS

Professionals work in many different kinds of situations; with individuals, groups, couples and teams as well as families. Some course members do not work directly with families for example, if they are managers. We are seeking to show them that systemic thinking is helpful whatever the context. We believe that the most helpful way to make training relevant is to be able to acknowledge and define our context as teachers, thereby facilitating course members to do the same throughout the course. We have found a number of techniques particularly useful in this connection:

1 The Professional Geneogram
We ask course participants to map their position within their agencies so that we, as teachers, can begin to address the problem of "I can do it on the course but not in my agency". The professional geneogram is the beginning of a process whereby a course

participant is able to identify the different systems of which he or she is a part and evolve the negotiation necessary to make the difference which will enable them to practise differently.

2. Peer Consultation

We link the training context with the agency context by asking course members to consult each other about their work. The effect is also to link each participant's context with all the other participants' contexts. They are then in a position to appreciate the similarities and differences which may enable them to change their own work patterns.

3 Case Material

Course participants submit cases for which they need new ideas. These are used for case discussion and a variety of role play exercises. Our suggested interventions around this case material have meaning within the teaching context and the views we have expressed. We need also to address the meaning for the course participants of taking views back to their agencies, as these new views may be challenged by others in their agencies. We have to negotiate around defining our responsibility in relation to the case and the course participants so as to free each course participant to use his or her skills in his or her own work context.

4 Agency Consultation

Whilst on the Course, participants provide many perceived problems in their agencies for discussion and we tend to encourage peer consultation on these issues, as yet another context in which it is possible to apply systemic thinking. A development of this work has been suggested by pleas from course participants like, "If only you could talk to my manager". We think that closer links between the training and agency contexts are the next step for us. For example, we could envisage negotiation with the agency around the participation of the prospective course participant just as we do when we negotiate the course itself with the host institution.

Chapter 2

SYSTEMATIC TEACHING PREPARATION

INTRODUCTION

In this section we hope to show how to generalize from the issues identified and discussed in Chapter 1 as these issues are specific to our Tavistock Course experience.

We are aware that some of the content may seem repetitive but want to show how similar content has different meaning when placed in particular context.

Systematic teaching preparation requires a teacher to attend to the following:

1. SETTING GOALS FOR THE COURSE

(a) Introductory Training

Goals for an Introductory Training might be for the teacher "to disseminate as much detailed information as possible" and for the course participant "to take away as much detailed information as possible".

On Introductory Courses participants want information but are not necessarily convinced of its value. Although this style of course is still available today, e.g., short term in-service courses, more course participants attend courses with more knowledge and request help to make the leap to put knowledge into practice. This has had a dramatic effect on the way teachers think and prepare.

Introductory Courses have had to be extended to cover the material: the increased commitment has led to requests from participants for qualifying certification. The professional bodies have responded with a serious attempt to administer the courses in order to sustain standards and ensure that clear objectives are met: this in turn has led to a demand for continued training. Job descriptions and requirements are being challenged and redefined.

(b) Goals for More Advanced Training

At this level of training, the goals appear to be different. The emphasis here is to continue to share and evaluate course participants' experience of applying family therapy, theory and practice. The courses have a higher practice component and can require a greater time commitment.

The goal of the teacher could be said to be "to provide an environment where family therapy skills and ideas from course participants can be developed within the framework of current theory and practice".

The goal of the course participants could be said to be "To evaluate therapy skills in a training group context where attention will be given to the development of technical expertise within the framework of current theory and practice".

(c) Some Key Goals for the Tavistock Courses

At the present time the following are offered as possible general goals for *all* courses:

1   To enable participants to reach a systemic explanation for how they can apply learning in their work contexts.

2   To enable a participant to organise the ideas that he/she has about family therapy theory and practice.

3   To enable the teacher and participant to become joined and agreed about a task, to enable the teacher to remain connected with a participant's specific needs.

4   To facilitate active participation of the course participant by presenting his/her own work to the group and using the group to test out new ways of working and to resolve difficult situations.

5   To enable the teacher to monitor the balance between stimulating the course member with new ideas and consolidating the material already covered.

6   To facilitate course participant's commitment to reading material prescribed on the course as well as material of their own choice.

7   To enable course participants to apply new learning and skills in their own agencies.

2 WHY DO YOU WANT TO TEACH?
In our view it is important that the teacher is clear about his/her own needs for professional development as a teacher in order for there to be a good fit between teacher and course participants. Mutual fulfilment enhances creativity at every level of teaching–learning-system and needs to be explicit and acknowledged.

Here are some reasons we have heard why clinicians want to teach:

1   Teaching can offer the clinician a platform where his/her ideas can be shared, challenged, stimulated and developed.

2   Teaching requires that the teacher keep up with the field (e.g., the 1989 Children Act, NHS White Paper, etc.). Curiosity and interest about the way legislation affects practice is a prerequisite for good teaching.

3   Sharing beliefs can sometimes include proselytising, i.e., hoping to convince others about the "good news" of this way of working. Some of these "others" might include teachers or course participants in key positions, colleagues (a co-therapist or a co-teacher) with whom the teacher hopes to be able to continue to work after the course.

4   Defining oneself as a teacher amongst clinician colleagues is often a way the teacher hopes for recognition of added competence.

5   Practising a skill which may be needed in the work-place; management in many Social Service Departments, Hospital Teams, Probation Service, Health Teams now run teaching events focused on staff development and may wish to recruit teachers for these events from the existing staff.

3 PROFESSIONAL NETWORKING

A most time consuming task at this stage is meeting with significant people in the system. Deciding with whom to negotiate; who to visit first; with whom to discuss what issues; ensuring that each member of the system is involved with your negotiations sufficiently to give you maximum negotiating space; corresponding with key people and others; all form part of the creative planning that will provide the framework for the course. Experience has so far shown that when difficulties arise before, during and after a course, the dilemmas can usually be located in this area rather than in the course content and delivery. What often feels like a questionably inordinate amount of time spent in this part of the process of teaching is usually time well invested and well worth the effort. Permission is needed from significant people in the system in order to create a context for change (Campbell and Draper, 1985).

Exploration of the teacher's context is perhaps the task most likely to maximise the teacher's manoeuvrability within the teaching event. We give an example of a teacher negotiating a teaching context in an agency where he is also employed:

Christine has been invited by her new training officer to set up an introductory course in family therapy. This was to be within the local authority for whom she worked as a level 3 social worker in a child guidance team. Christine was an advanced trained family therapist and was practising systemic work within the service. The clinic where she was placed had excellent facilities to accommodate such a course. She was concerned about some of the possible tensions that could arise about her running the course, but abandoned these in the belief that she was safeguarded since the invitation stemmed from management level.

It was not long before Christine discovered herself struggling with what she would earlier have predicted to be minor details.

(i)   The head of the team indicated that the accommodation in the Clinic might not always be available for the course.

(ii) The training officer did not produce the advertising on time and so the starting date was challenged.

(iii) Prospective trainees declared their commitment to the course verbally, but were not filling in the application forms.

(iv) Christine's direct line management were concerned about the time commitment.

(v)   The Clinic was ambivalent about the incursion into Christine's clinic time. To Christine's consternation, these and other issues began to emerge and she challenged the viability of the task in the face of what seemed considerable opposition. Christine requested supervision before abandoning the task. The tasks within supervision were:

(a) To define the significant teaching context,

and

(b) to examine Christine's position in that system.

The effect of this work was to shift Christine's perspective of the system and help her explore different alternatives for herself to enable the teaching experience to take place. Christine discovered others who would be affected by her teaching the course, e.g., a colleague from another clinic who had been to the same course. She had planned to attend as a course member. Christine revised this with an invitation to her to contribute to the teaching.

She discovered the significance of the course to different members of her own team and this led to her considering involving them in the course in ways that would address the needs of the Clinic more favourably, e.g., the Director of the Clinic hosted the inaugural meeting and was asked to contribute to the input. This latter invitation was in fact not taken up, but he talked of the course with much pride as a Clinic resource.

Christine discovered the importance of connecting the training officer to the event ensuring that the course had an impact on Training Provision in the locality. This assisted the smoother running of the course and enabled co-operation at a wider level.

Christine ensured that her immediate line manager was invited to participate in the inaugural event as well as involving her, together with other key people in his teaching network, in evaluative procedures throughout the course.

Defining the teaching context helped Christine find herself able to operate from different positions in the system. She appreciated not only the immediate manoeuvrability this offered her, but also how this was going to have to continue for the duration of the course. Most interesting of all, was the extent to which she involved the entire network in her teaching event, yet experienced herself astonishingly in charge of the training task and sufficiently manoeuvrable to enjoy it.

This example shows how necessary it is to understand the context within which one is teaching. The significant system needs to be defined. As many members as possible of organisations affected in any way by running of the course need to be identified and addressed accordingly and respectfully.

4 SELECTING A SUPERVISOR OR CONSULTANT
Select a supervisor for your teaching–learning-system. In order to be most useful, it is recommended that defining the teaching context be done within this framework. This will ensure that, amongst the teaching issues, the network issues will continue to be addressed throughout the running of the course.

5 CONSUMER RESEARCH
Whether you have decided to teach a new course or been invited

to teach an already established course, it is important that you are convinced there is a real need for the course you envisage. Where the course you are teaching or being asked to teach has an established history, the assurances are easier to find. These may come from informal gatherings from past candidates, existing trainers of the course, large application lists and even formal follow-up studies of that course.

Where the course is a new one, it is more difficult and requires considerably more research on the part of the teacher to confirm a hunch which is often based on observations and experience in another context. For example – consider this popular notion.

The GP might well be more able to help those patients suffering from stress if he/she had more systemic perspectives about family life.

This might lead to setting up a course for GPs. The general premise might well appear to generate considerable support from other systemic practitioners who might be willing to share this notion. It is most disappointing when there is little response to an invitation or advertising to attend such an event.

5.1 How can this be avoided ?
Research your market place thoroughly, being sure that what you plan to offer has a wider context within which it can be relevant. Then ask, "What would a course have to offer so that systemic ideas would be presented to the GP in such a way that it would fit with the medical service he/she provides?"

The teaching network is first identified. Thereafter, informal discussion is a most useful resource, but rarely sufficient on its own. In addition to meetings with the key people in the network, marketing is recommended with possible supervisors and participants. This could take the form of a formal meeting, questionnaire or mini-course. It is from these careful marketing procedures that creative course design emerges.

It is useful to note that even where courses are well established, it is necessary to continue to check the existing format with the market place to enable an on-going fit between teachers, teaching and participants' needs.

6 SELECTION OF COURSE PARTICIPANTS
Often, the first two issues that seem clear are for whom the

course is intended and for how many it will cater. As with the rest of the planning, the definition of the teaching network is usually built around the anticipated membership of the proposed course.

If the course is interdisciplinary, psychologists, field and residential social workers, nurses, psychiatrists and members of other helping professions along with supervisors and managers from these settings, are eligible to apply. Participants are expected to have two years post-qualifying experience and to be currently working with families.

Once the format of the course is clarified and the stage of participant selection is once again addressed, it is not uncommon for these original parameters to be challenged, e.g., whilst the course might have originally been planned to cater for social workers from a particular area, consideration may now have to be given to applicants from another area in order to draw on a large enough constituency.

Inevitably, applications do come from candidates who do not appear to meet the selection criteria. Whether you decide to take them or not depends on the implications of their participation for the teaching process and other course participants' learning. You might choose to interview students where you have some concern; and in some situations selection interviewing seems to enhance the participants' commitment to the course.

7 APPLICATION FORMS

Application forms are usually part of the expected administration for courses where selection is a feature and payments are part of the contract. These vary in design and their content is influenced by the nature of the course.

When courses are offered to departments for in-service programmes/staff development, application forms are often discounted as unnecessary. It does, however, seem that application forms assist the definition of the participants' commitment to the course. A formal application procedure also has the effect of conveying the priority given to the course by the sponsoring management. Some questions that could be included on applications forms are:

1   As far as you can predict, would your work commitments allow you the time to attend the course on a regular basis?

2   What might be a particular area you would like to pursue in the group that particularly interests you in your work?

3   How would you see your career developing over the next five years?

4   Where in your agency do you get support for your family work?

8 RESOURCING THE COURSE

Resourcing the course becomes inextricably interwoven with the success of the teaching–learning process. Some proposed costing considerations:

1   Teacher's fee (Travel costs and administration time considered here).

2   Accommodation costs.

3   Facilities for refreshments.

4   Advertising.

5   General Secretarial costs (e.g., mail out to course participants, letters to people in the network, handout material for the course itself, photocopying facility, etc.).

6   Cost of audio-visual equipment.

7   Cost of possible guest teacher.

8   Bursaries where possible.

9   Cost of a reading facility for students, e.g., library, books or journals.

10   Supervisors' fees.

When courses run on too fine a budget, the aims and goals of the course become constrained. The teacher runs the risk of working within a negative feedback loop. Participants then experience confirmation of their worst suspicions about mediocrity of practice related to poor provision.

9 SYLLABUS PLANNING
How do you decide what to teach?
The content will be influenced by the aims and objectives of the course. The knowledge base is easier to select where the course is agency and/or discipline specific. When the course is of longer duration, options broaden and selecting the knowledge base becomes more complicated as well as offering more potential.

Teachers often plan a syllabus reflecting successful ways they have learned. Teachers usually add their own areas of special interest as well as other important developments in the field and sponsoring agencies' requirements.

Whether to present one or more family therapy models *or* to focus mostly on the shift from linear thinking to circular *or* to present one model of working only, has become a popular debate. When asked what they preferred, in a survey we conducted, most course participants wanted more than one family systems approach clarified at the introductory level.

The key issue is that the course content selected by the teacher is distinctive and distinguished by the way the content fits with the work contexts of course participants. The fact that this is developed within the teaching–learning-system and with supervision, also contributes to the way one set of course contents is distinguished from another.

Examples of a course outline has been included in Appendix I. We hope you will use and adapt such ideas and that your course syllabuses will be distinctive to your course context and reflect your own creativity as teachers.

Reading material was given the highest rating of all as a teaching 'method' in our survey. Participants wanted more material and extra time to read it. The implication for us is that time put into preparing coherent reading lists and identifying papers that support the theoretical and technical input is time well spent.

Reading lists can comprise a mixture of books and journal articles. The lists could be divided into prescribed reading and recommended reading indicating which material is essential. This assists trainees to organise their reading time and to decide what to buy if they can and want to.

Depending on the course, reading lists will differ in length.

Some basic principles apply:

(a)   Include some early seminal writings and some contemporary publications.

(b)   Reading lists are best divided into sections indicating the connection to a specific theory or relevant to a topic, e.g., child sexual abuse, family life cycle, adult psychiatric patients, the elderly, etc. This can be done for each term for a full year.

(c)   Whilst it is important to offer a comprehensive list, it should be remembered that too extensive a list is often daunting and unrealistic for course participants.

(d)   Some additional reading that addresses course participants' feedback to teachers should be offered during the course. This should be easily manageable for participants as a short additional paper is usually read with enthusiasm.

Making sure the reading is accessible, not only for purchase but for loan too, assists the extent to which people supplement the theory presented to them. By making it clear that reading is a course requirement, more time is available in the teaching sessions for experiential learning.

Several reading lists have been included in Appendix II illustrating the above points.

10 PLANNING THE FIRST SESSION

This is often experienced as an awesome task. Much is unknown and there is always uncertainty about the extent to which you can offer the experience that you would hope for as a new course participant.

At this point, very specific planning and time of teacher's input is usually helpful. The session outline can even be pedantically organised (see example of session plan in the Appendix).

The first session should address a number of different topics that do not arise in the same way at any other time on the course.

(a) Introduction to the Course

It has been our practice to write to all participants about one week prior to the first course meeting confirming the starting date, the meeting place and sometimes including a reading list (see Appendix) . This seems to help create the context and is the teacher's first step towards engagement with the whole group.

Preparing the room, arranging seating and organising your own position are interventions that create the first feedback from the course participants. The experience of being seated with the group for the first time can be quite overwhelming and might require a deep breath or two before you continue whether you are a teacher or a course participant. What next?

Outlining the history and context of the course itself is necessary so that participants can experience their position within this system. Your own position in the system and other key teaching colleagues would be defined. If other teachers are to participate in the course from time to time, it is useful to introduce them by name at least (if not in person) to the course at the first meeting. Teacher's aims and objectives should be shared with participants so that they know what is expected of them on the course, e.g., reading, paired working, writing tasks, etc. An over-view of the course content should be offered. Some teachers prefer to offer a course outline at this stage. Others find this a constraint as it seems to reduce flexibility as well as the ability to alter the course in response to feedback. Reading lists may be handed out, if they have not already been posted to participants.

(b) Group Introductions
This is an important part of the beginning of the course. There are a number of popular ways to introduce group members to each other, for example:

1   After discussion with your neighbour, you could introduce him/her to the group.

2   Ask each participant to offer their name, their work context and what has prompted them to apply for the course.

3   Name tags could be offered to the group and intermingling could be prescribed, permitting each person to ask one question only before moving on to the next person. This could be randomly fed back in the large group.

(c) General Administration
Included here are, for example:

1   Name and address lists. It is recommended that permission be asked of the group before these can be circulated.

2   Whether photocopying facilities are available or not.

3   Arranging for someone to take notes for the group (usually something specific) at each session, e.g., three new ideas, one issue you struggled with, etc.

4   Use of tapes.

5   Confidentiality issues.

6   Car Parking.

7   Timetable and punctuality.

8   Refreshments, if any.

A comprehensive schedule would be too numerous to list and will be dictated by the course and its context. The careful management of administration issues from the outset sets the tone of the event and offers a containing environment within which to learn. It is customary to reserve a small slot for administrative issues at each teaching session through the course.

(d) Planning coffee time in the session
This often becomes an important part of the course ritual and can be arranged to help in setting a framework for the session. Coffee break can divide a session into two separate halves or coffee at the start of a session can have a convening effect and allows the session to be continuous.

(e) Ensuring participants leave the first session with "hope" for next time
This is true for all sessions, but particularly important in this first session and can be achieved by keeping the balance between presenting theory and then practising its application with the group. A new concept embedded into some skills practice is often an important intervention to ensure the immediate relevance of the course to the trainees' work setting.

It is equally necessary to remember to plan some way in which the session will connect with the next session, e.g., a brief skills task to practise; promise of a video to continue to illustrate the issues of the first session or a reading task.

11 THE SECOND SESSION TOWARDS THE MID PHASE OF THE COURSE

Not infrequently, the first session ends with considerable relief and thrill. For the teacher the course is up and running. The teaching in the first session has the immediate effect of creating connections in the teaching–learning-system and the teacher's capacity to respond to feedback is tested.

In contrast to the first, the second session, mirroring the therapeutic process, often feels like a hard slog. The session can feel much longer than the first since much less time is taken with administrative issues. Although motivation is still high, the prospect for the teacher of so many more sessions to prepare for can feel daunting at this point and it is almost impossible to envisage enough energy to complete the whole course.

Some general issues characteristic of this part of the developing course are:

(a)   A great deal of preparation on the part of the teacher. This is not only a matter of becoming familiar with the theoretical material selected for teaching, but also grappling with designing ways to assist the group to integrate the concepts experientially. This remains a constant task for each session. You prepare a session, you teach that session and then find yourself with the preparation again. It is in the supervision framework that you are helped to think at least three sessions ahead as a way of clearing a path forward.

(b)   At this stage, you are receiving and processing the feedback as best you can and vigilance here with the aid of supervision (usually more frequent at this stage of the course) is invaluable. Mistakes are made in spite of all efforts and can seem almost irretrievable, e.g., feeling unhappy about a participant's participation in a role play and then he/she fails to attend the next session; a boring theoretical presentation; being challenged by a group member and feeling uncomfortable about the response; timing your session badly.

(c)   As you complete about a third of the course, you will discover you have begun to relax as participants begin to grapple with the content and the group process feels less predominant. You begin to recognise that you have a wider margin for errors than initially anticipated and your prospects of survival have improved. There are after all only *good enough* teachers no *perfect* ones.

d)   You begin to admire the enthusiasm of the participants and this response allows you to address issues in the group differently, e.g., critical feedback need no longer be misconstrued as your having presented the material poorly. The enthusiasm permeates the whole system and the group seems to learn quickly.

(e)   About mid-way through the course, attendances seem to become less stable with one or two more people away than usual. Others might express fatigue in relation to their jobs and this is often used as a way of justifying not having been able to complete homework tasks (no matter how small). This always comes as a surprise and is often quite sudden. It is possible that participants reach a point of saturation and the pace of learning needs to change. The feedback is clear and can be confused with course participants' resistance. This is the time you have been waiting for, since you too can slow down and join with the group as they integrate the ideas they have heard. At this point it is useful to avoid homework tasks, extra reading and the choice of material needs to be simple enough to enjoy. A nice time for discussion about participants' own work contexts and the effect of their being on a course within their agencies. A kind of review. This can be of a short duration (one session) or could extend over into two or three sessions but needs careful monitoring so that the group does not lose its momentum. It could be a question of practising with "old" material to ensure that what might look like "mid-course blues" is recognised as a necessary plateau to allow participants to stabilise their ideas.

12 MID PHASE OF THE COURSE AND TOWARDS THE END
The momentum increases less obviously. New issues begin to be raised by the group particularly related to the dilemmas about

putting ideas into practice. As members begin to get positive feedback from their own practice, their curiosity increases and the course enters a new phase.

What are the characteristics from here to the end?

(a)   By now, the group has become an intimate resource group. The course becomes a safe place to try more personalised tasks, where there are greater risks from both the trainer and the participants' point of view.

The group will probably be sharing informal reading and even be thinking about work tasks (pairing) outside of the session. Course participants will have taken a number of risks in their agencies, will have brought homework for review and will have brought work dilemmas for discussion in the training.

(b)   At a time when the group seems to want more again, an element of teacher fatigue often enters. Finding ways through this is essential. You will need to limit your own input for a while by, e.g., inviting more from the group; video watching; bringing in an outside teacher, etc. Supervision is important at this stage to help move your concentration towards ending issues with which it is easy to engage.

(c)   About two-thirds of the way through the course, ending issues need to be addressed. Course participants begin to ask about life after the course and further training. Evaluation and accreditation become aspects for discussion as they hypothesise about the continuing impact of the course on their practice.

(d)   Final rituals are planned well in advance. These rituals will address not only the connection between the participants and the teacher, but also the entire teaching–learning-system. This can be planned in different ways. Some courses have held a drinks party to which all participants have been invited; others have leaned on the teacher to address this in separate groupings. Ritual endings anticipating loss and acknowledging resistance to a final punctuation are important to the success (and paradoxically) to the likely continued learning of course participants. Reunion meetings or reviews some six months after the course are often suggested and are usually interesting. Professional networking amongst course participants and between participants and teachers is important as it is an entry to future training possibilities. It allows for a positive definition of the completed course confirming participants' professional evolution in their work places. An example of professional networking could be an attempt to evaluate the participant's progress in the agency with a before/after questionnaire, sharing the results by personal interview/letter with key people in the agency and the participants themselves.

13 CONCLUSION

This chapter has attempted to systemically review some of the important features of setting up and running a course. The issues that have been highlighted are:

(a)   the attention to the teaching context that includes teachers, participants and the wider teaching and training environment;

(b)   the attention to detail at the point of determining objectives for a course; defining what it is you want to teach and designing the content of the course to accommodate this;

(c)   some detail about first sessions; and,

(d)   an overview of the life of the course from beginning to the mid-phase and then to the end.

All these issues contribute to the excitement and pleasure of an evolving teaching–learning-system. Many participants have continued in further study or have redefined their job descriptions since the course. Many teachers have gone on to evaluate their own clinical contributions in the form of research and publication and agencies and organisations continue to support in-house training ventures and send staff to outside courses.

There is both pleasure and pain in teaching. By pointing out some of our difficulties and responses to these situations, we hope we can offer other teachers the prospect of a smoother path.

Chapter 3

TEACHING THEORY & SKILLS PRACTICE

1. AN INTRODUCTION TO THE EXERCISES

We give below some general guide-lines for the use of role play, sculpting and video. These are universal modes of teaching and are integral to many of our exercises. We think they deserve special mention to enable teachers to maximise the learning possibilities of exercises.

2. THE USE OF ROLE PLAY

It is important for trainees to get the feel of interviewing a family without the ethical problems of treating real clients as guinea pigs, yet giving them a chance of taking risks in trying out new ideas in a relatively safe context. We have come to see role play as not only a specific technique but also a general principle of teaching practice skills. It is an effective means for trainees to develop their skills and can often be far more involving than watching videotape of a real family. Course participants receive instant feedback either in their role as therapist or as a family member and realise what interventions they found helpful or unhelpful. We have found, however, that role play needs as careful thought and preparation as real therapy. On account of its central position in training, we have chosen to emphasise its format and offer some general guidelines to the teacher embarking on the use of role play in teaching.

(a) Preparation for role play
The possibilities are as follows:

Clients chosen from a course participant's own caseload
This is useful when the group has got to the stage of wanting to consult to each other on how to get themselves "unstuck" in their work with a particular family. In this case, it can be helpful to ask the person presenting the case to remain as an observer to the role play, adding their comments at the end. If they join in, either as a family member or as a member of the therapy team, there is always the risk that they will influence the proceedings too much with their own script and thereby get "more of the same", rather than fresh ideas for future work.

Clients chosen from the teacher's own case load
This has the advantage of the above method of being drawn from real life but distanced from the experience of the course participants and therefore may allow them to focus on the material for skills practice without getting too drawn into content issues. There is, however, the risk that the course participants may become too interested in the work of the teacher with the family and unless it is the intention to show something of this work (e.g., by showing videotape of particular parts of the therapy) it may introduce a competitive or de-skilling dimension which may not be desirable at that point.

Course participants who will simulate a family
can be asked to"invent themselves" as a family
Either taking time beforehand to develop a script for themselves or else inventing it as they go along in *ad hoc* fashion. This can be a useful approach when the focus of the exercise is purely skills practice. For example, trying out different types of questioning. It frees the course participants from too many feelings of responsibility for the case and, particularly in the case of an *ad hoc* family, gives them the experience of being fast on their feet in response to the feedback.

It is important to give those members not
involved in the role play specific tasks as observers
For example, to describe the patterns established between family
and therapist: to develop hypotheses, questions and an intervention in parallel with the therapy team. The observer group
will need to be given space to feed back on their work. Their
comments can often be some of the most illuminating on the
therapeutic process and act, to a certain extent, as a consultation
to both the therapy team and the teacher. It also offers group
members the opportunity of exploring involvement in the
therapeutic process at a different level than role play family
member or therapist alternatives. This can be a valuable
experience of being meta. The decision on which methods to
choose needs to go hand in hand with the planning of the
exercise as a whole, and considers the purpose of the exercise in
the development of the course participants' learning These
issues will be addressed in the description of exercises where
role play is involved.

(b) Conduct of role play

There is a tendency for trainees to be very effective playing the
parts of clients. In some cases, this can make it difficult for the
therapy team. Role play clients can attempt to "beat the
therapist", which can sometimes destroy fragile confidence in
course participants who are in role as therapists. The teacher
needs to be sensitive to this and avoid helping the therapy team
in such a way as to escalate the problem. It is always helpful if
the exercise can be organised so as to give the 'family' a chance
to be the therapy team as well, as this can introduce an appropriate sense of humility! Another approach we have used when
we have had two parallel groups is to pair a therapy team from
one group with a role play family from the other group and vice
versa. This tends to lend a degree of unfamiliarity which
simulates a meeting with a real family. It also allows for more
risk taking in the therapy team which is not working with
members of their own group; they seem to worry less about
challenging members of another group.

(c) Ending the role play

There are many different ways of ending a role play that address
the powerful effect of simulating family roles. We have used the
following methods:

1.   Each member of the role play family can say who they
     were in the family, then say one way in which they identify
     with that family member and one way in which they are
     different. They can then conclude with saying who they
     really are in their professional role and change places in the
     room, making a conscious effort to change their body
     posture.

2.   As above, but in place of the second step, they can describe
     what they did at the weekend.

We find it important to devote time to de-roling and ending
the role play, especially if it comes at the end of the session, as
there is a risk of trainees taking their roles home with them and
perhaps not wanting to come back next time as a result!

3. THE USE OF SCULPTING
This is a useful technique in which role play is encapsulated as if
it were a single frame of a film. The group participant presenting
a family can be asked to place other group members in body
positions and in relation to one another as he or she sees the
attitudes and relationships in the family forming a "living
tableau". This is usually a static and silent representation of a
family structure and can be used both therapeutically and for
teaching purposes. The sculpture can be taken into movement to
illustrate the effects of change on the system. For example, one
might ask a particular family member to move others into
positions which would feel more comfortable and explore the
effects by asking other family members how they feel. One
might chose to use a sculpture rather than a role play as it slows
down interactions and offers time for observation. It is
particularly useful for studying very large systems, such as
agency networks. With clients it is a powerful way to enable
people to say how they want things to change and have a
physical experience of what are the gains and losses in bringing
about change.

4. THE USE OF VIDEO
Video supervision and feedback is becoming more accepted as a
training tool and we view it as being as important as role play,
hence its special mention here. The value of a teacher/super-
visor being able to see and comment on what course members

actually did needs no amplification.

We have found that it is tricky getting the timing right in showing videotape of other therapists. People find it difficult not to get drawn into family content even if they have been asked to look solely at process. Watching too much videotape can also be soporific. We try to maximise its effectiveness by showing only about 10 minutes of tape at a time. If we are showing a whole session, we would break it up into 10 minute sections, with breaks for discussion, hypothesis-making and set tasks for observation in between. In this way, trainees are enabled to maintain concentration and distance from content issues. We list here a number of ways we have used video as part of teaching:

O   showing videotape of other therapists at work for demonstration purposes or as an adjunct to theoretical presentations by the teacher;

O   making tapes with participants themselves engaged in exercises, especially role play;

O   making tapes of outside speakers;

O   asking people to bring in tapes made in their agencies;

O   tape review for skills training;

O   tape review as a form of supervision;

O   tape review as a form of evaluation.

We hope that these uses will be integrated in the examples of exercises that follow.

5. THE TEACHING EXERCISES
We have organised the exercises into three sections:

O   Structural Family Therapy

O   Strategic Family Therapy

O   Milan Systemic Family Therapy

Whilst we have tried to address variations within these approaches, particularly in the section on *Strategic Family Therapy*, our teaching has been structured around the three distinct models upon which most family therapy practice is based. We have found that this helps course participants to understand the fundamental theoretical differences between the approaches. They are then more able to find a coherent theoretical stance with which they feel comfortable and to go on to develop the relevant skills which flow from it in their own practice.

In presenting our exercises in this way, we do not aim to cover all the theoretical and practice issues associated with each model, nor do we give adequate coverage to other models, but merely share our ideas. We hope to give other teachers some examples of our "tried and true" exercises which they might find useful and also act as a stimulus to their own creativity.

Each exercise is presented in the following format:

a)   *An introduction* covering the uses of the exercise at various points in the training of family therapists and feedback we have received about its effectiveness.

b)   *A statement of the aim* of the exercise.

c)   *A step by step description* of the exercise, so the reader can carry it out with a teaching group.

d)   *Instructions for closing the exercise* so as to create a coherent experience.

e)   *Further suggestions* for developing the exercise in different directions and how to connect it to other teaching material so as to create a balanced teaching event.

f)   *A maximum of three relevant references* to the literature. This is by no means comprehensive and should be regarded as the minimum necessary preparation to address the exercises suggested.

g)   *Ratings* in the form of symbols to represent our evaluation of the exercise in terms of preparation time, time for the exercise itself and level of experience required of participants.

6. KEY TO SYMBOLS
Of course there is a personal bias in the way we have assigned the exercises. Our assessments are not definitive and mostly relevant in relation to our own experience. We hope people will challenge our judgement and refine the exercises accordingly.

(a) Preparation Time

Quick to prepare

Takes up to 1 hour

Time consuming

(b) Minimum Time to carry out exercise
As indicated by the clock, e.g.

15 mins

30 mins

45 mins

1 hour, etc.,

N.B. We have given minimum times, but people can take differing amounts of time to complete them, depending on the feedback from the teaching group.

The time indicated does not include time for theoretical presentation of ideas needed to be able to embark upon the exercise. The assumption is that all these exercises are presented in the context of theoretical issues.

(c) Level of Experience in Course Participants

Beginners   ✓

Intermediate   ✓ ✓

Advanced   ✓ ✓ ✓

Any Level   ✓ ✓ ✓ ✓

Chapter 4

Structural Family Therapy:

TEACHING EXERCISES

Structural Family Therapy

Introduction

These exercises are almost exclusively based on the work of Minuchin as we would often start our teaching on family therapy models by studying the structural family therapy model via his writing and practice. In our experience, course participants find it easier to begin with this model as it often relates closely to their own current practice and the development of family therapy practice in this country – and then to move on to other models. A further point is that the theory and relevant skills associated with this model are clearly and simply presented in Minuchin's writing.

Minuchin describes the structural family therapist's task as the transformation of the family into a more effectively functioning group, rather than the manipulation of individual family members. He or she does this by becoming a part of the family system in various ways (joining and engaging) in order to understand the family structure. Minuchin's model or family structure involves a model of the family as a set of sub-systems (parental sub-system, child sub-system) between which are boundaries, symbolic relationship markers which, if not present can lead to ineffective functioning or dysfunction. The development of a dysfunction is seen as the way a family maintains a balance or homoeostasis between its constituent parts, which might otherwise be threatened by disintegration at times of a need for developmental changes in the family system. Minuchin encourages therapists to develop visual representations of their observations of family structure in the form of maps.

Minuchin's method of intervention involves restructuring the family into a more effectively functioning group so that the dysfunction disappears and the symptom is no longer necessary. He uses various techniques to achieve this and our exercises deal with some of them:

Unbalancing	Changing the hierarchical relationship of members of a sub-system;
Promoting Enactment	Asking family members to demonstrate how they relate to one another, as a prelude to suggesting different patterns of interaction;
Intensification	Amplifying and exaggerating a dysfunctional interaction as a challenge to the existing structure;
Complementarity	Extending the family's understanding of its dilemma by exploring many interactions affected by the dysfunction or the "whole dance"; and
Reframing	Providing alternative explanations for the family problem relating to its function in maintaining homoeostasis in the system.

Exercise 1:

JOINING AND ENGAGING: STARTING OFF

INTRODUCTION

Minuchin considers it important for the family therapist to become a part of the family system in order to explore and experience for himself or herself the family structure which gives rise to the dysfunction. He calls this process joining and it is the means by which the therapist connects with or engages the family in the therapeutic process. He describes different positions of joining and we think it is important that course participants practise these different ways. Minuchin says that the therapist's job as a healer requires him or her to be able to join a family in particular ways but he or she "must also have the skills to un-join, then rejoin in a differentiated way – and there's the rub!" (Minuchin, 1982, p. 30).

In the introduction to this exercise with the group, it is important to clarify each of the joining positions, Minuchin's rationale for joining in the broader context of his therapeutic model and some of the dilemmas raised by Minuchin in attempting these techniques. This is an easy exercise to organise and for trainees to execute competently. It presents good opportunity for complimenting people's practice at a time when they may be feeling nervous about coming on a course.

Aim: Practising technique of joining.

Task:

1.   The group can be divided into three groups.

2.   Each group needs to choose two people to role play a couple to be interviewed.

3.   Each group would be allocated a joining position, i.e., close position, medium position or disengaged position and

would be asked, one at a time, to perform a five minute interview with the couple in the group in front of the large group.

Closing the Exercise

General feedback and group discussion on some of the problems raised by joining techniques, for example working with people it is not easy to join with because of "different chemistry".

Further Suggestions

You could take feedback immediately after each interview or hold it until the closing discussion. It is important the exercise does not go on too long as other ideas about the interviewing process need to be introduced to ensure joining in itself does not become the perceived therapeutic process. If you have a smaller group, the same group might need to carry out the three different joining positions. You may also need three different families as well and could circulate membership of therapist and role play members.

Reading

Burnham, J. (1986) *Family Therapy, First Steps Towards a Systemic Approach*. Tavistock: London.
Convening, Preparation and Interviewing 1,
Chapters 5, 6 & 7.

Haley, J. (1987) *Problem Solving Therapy*. Jossey-Bass: San Francisco. "Conducting the First Interview" Chapter 1.

Minuchin, S. and Fishman, H. (1981) *Family Therapy Techniques*. Harvard University Press: Cambridge, Mass.

Ratings

Preparation Time:

Minimum Time Necessary:

Level of Experience Needed: ✓

Exercise 2:

OBSERVING BOUNDARIES

INTRODUCTION

A theoretical introduction to Minuchin's model of family structure and the notion of boundaries between family sub-systems is
necessary to help people understand what they are looking for.
Minuchin presents this very clearly and participants generally
find it easy to key into the idea of boundaries and will probably
be able to make astute observations on the family quite quickly.

Aim: Understanding of family structure, particularly the
notion of boundaries.

Task

1.   The teacher can present information about a family, e.g.,
      mother and father with 16 year old girl and 12 year old
      school refusing boy. Mother is ambivalent about the school
      (implicitly supporting her son's school refusal) whilst
      father is trying to get him back to school.

2.   The group can be asked to take family roles and that of the
      therapist. The rest of the group is asked to observe.

3.   The teacher interviews the family with a member of the
      group as co-therapist whilst the observers have the task of
      making notes about the family structure. They are
      particularly asked to look for interactions which indicate
      how relationships are organised into sub-systems. They
      might be given a few prompt questions such as:

      Who communicates with who in the family?
      Which members are closest to one another?
      Are any members excluded?
      Who supports who in the family?, etc.

Closing the Exercise
The teacher can encourage the observers to define the boundaries between the sub-systems and to check their observations with the family

Further Suggestions

1. The group can attempt to make a diagrammatic representation of the family by drawing it on a board or flip-chart.

2. This exercise could include attempts by the therapist to change the boundaries during the role play and see what the observers notice.

3. Group members can observe videotape of a structural therapist at work and attempt to identify the boundaries in the family and what they think the therapist is doing.

Reading
Minuchin, S. (1982) *Families and Family Therapy.*
        Tavistock: London
        Chapters 3 and 5

Will, D. and Wrate, R.M. (1985) *Integrated Family Therapy.*
        Tavistock: London, and N.Y.
        Chapter 3, pp. 28–36.

Ratings
Preparation Time:

Minimum Time Necessary:

Level of Experience Needed: ✓

Exercise 3:

ILLUSTRATING THE HOMOEOSTATIC TENDENCIES OF A FAMILY SYSTEM

INTRODUCTION

Minuchin describes the family as a system striving for homoeostasis or balance amongst its constituent parts in the face of demands for change, for example the need for parents to behave differently towards their children as they grow up. The development of a dysfunction is seen as a product of the family striving to remain the same despite a need for change. For this reason families also resist therapeutic attempts to bring about change. This core concept is now referred to as homoeostatic tendencies within the system. This exercise gives participants an opportunity to see and experience the power of these homoeostatic tendencies. They are usually surprised at how predictable the pattern becomes for them and has immediate effect on their perception of themselves as therapists.

Aim: Exploration of the homoeostatic tendencies of a family system.

Task

1.   Some group members can devise a role play family. This should be an impromptu family group, not a case known to the group or the teacher.

2.   Someone from the group is asked to enact a journalist who is writing an article about the family as follows:

    Part 1: This journalist is to interview the family to gather information about them, observed by other members of the group.
    Part 2: The family divorces, family breaks down; both partners re-marry. The journalist interviews them 6 months later.

Throughout Part 1 and 2, the teacher needs to continue to engage the group by continually making comments about what they observe about the family. The comments are about the homoeostatic or system-maintaining properties and predictability of the families. Questions about what participants think might happen next are fun if asked during the process.

Closing the Exercise
The teacher should draw together the most important observations, paying particular attention to the loyalty to the original family system.

Further Suggestions
1. This is an interesting exercise which allows the teacher to contribute to the interaction in such a way as to underline key ideas on unchanging structures, comments on loyalty to the old system in step-families and predictability.

2. As a variation group members could observe a videotape of a structural family therapist at work and attempt to identify repetitive and predictable patterns of interaction.

Reading
Gorell Barnes, G. (1964) *Working with Families.* Macmillan Education Ltd., British Association of Social Workers, Chapter 2.

Minuchin, S. and Fishman, H.C. (1981) *Family Therapy Techniques.* Harvard University Press: Cambridge, Mass. Chapter 2, pp. 11–27.

Skynner, R. (1982) Framework for viewing the family as a system. In Bentovim, A. *et al.* (Eds) *Family Therapy: Complementary Frameworks of Theory and Practice.* Vol. 1.

Ratings
Preparation Time: 📖 📖

Minimum Time Necessary: ◑

Level of Experience Needed: ✓

Exercise 4:

FAMILY STRUCTURE FROM DRAWINGS

INTRODUCTION

A pictorial representation of the family is static and represents a moment in time in family life. It is useful in helping trainees to observe and understand the structural components in a family as described by Minuchin. The expectation of artistic skill is limited!

The exercise is based on adapting and expanding the use of Kinetic Family Drawings (K. F. D.). In this exercise, the clinical usefulness of drawings of the family is explored. We share the hope of the authors of K. F. D. that drawings speak for themselves and in this sense, we feel able to adapt it to this context. Their interpretive manual is most useful.

This is an exercise which works well with a small group of up to 8 people and can best be organised by sitting around a table in the manner of a working party. You need to equip yourself with paper and coloured felt-tip pens, pencils, etc.

Aim: Understanding the family as a structure.

The Task

1.   The group members can be asked to sit together around a table and are given the instruction, "Draw a picture of everyone in a family doing something". They can be given the option of drawing their own family or a family they might be working with.

2.   The drawings can be collected in a pile and shuffled. The teacher can then give them out at random to members of the group ensuring anonymity so that all the material can be sensitively handled. It is important that no-one finishes up with their own drawing.

3.   The group can be asked to make general structural interpretations from the drawings. There are different ways to do it:

    (a)   general group feedback
    (b)   pairs to share observations
    (c)   ask people to look for specific observations, for example, who is closest to whom?

Closing the Exercise
The teacher can begin a discussion on how people can use what they observe from two dimensional representations of the family in their therapeutic work. The teacher could ask people for a hypothesis they might have had about a family based on the drawing.

Further Suggestions
This is the sort of exercise which can be done spontaneously in a short space of time, say if video equipment has broken down or if members of the group are away leaving a smaller group than usual, so that the ones who do come have a treat!

    This is an exercise which can also be given as a homework task.

Reading
Burns, R.C. and Kaufman, S.H. (1972) *Actions, Styles and Symbols in Kinetic Family Drawings (K. F. D.).* Butterworths: London.

Minuchin, S. (1982) *Families and Family Therapy.* Tavistock: London.

Wilkinson, S. (1985) Drawing up Boundaries: A technique. *Journal of Family Therapy* 7, 2, pp. 99–112.

Ratings
Preparation Time:

Minimum Time Necessary:

Level of Experience Needed:

Exercise 5:

MAPPING

INTRODUCTION

Minuchin encourages therapists to record their observations of family structure in the form of a map or visual symbolic representation of family structure using certain mapping conventions (Minuchin, 1982, p. 53). This exercise is usually offered near the beginning of a presentation of Structural Family Therapy since it is such a useful technique for clarifying thinking about family problems. It offers a perspective on the family at a particular moment in time and the direction for therapeutic intervention is indicated. It is most useful for case recording.

Aim: Introduction of the technique of mapping and its conventions.

Task

1.   The teacher can write up on the board (or use handout) Minuchin's mapping conventions

2.   At this point, the teacher has several choices:

(a)   observe a family on tape;

(b)   ask the group to present a family from case material;

(c)   role play an impromptu family ;

(d)   sculpt a family for observation.

3.   In pairs or threes, the group can be asked to map the family according to Minuchin's guidelines. The teacher can go from group to group offering help if it is needed.

Closing the Exercise
The teacher can ask people to elect their focus for intervention for the next session, based on the maps people have made.

Further Suggestions
The mapping can be given as a homework task. It can be used with organisations as well as families, e.g., participants' own agencies.

Reading
Minuchin, S. (1974) *Families and Family Therapy.* Tavistock: London. Chapters 3 and 5.

Ratings
Preparation Time:

Minimum Time Necessary:

Level of Experience Needed:

Exercise 6:

OBSERVING DYSFUNCTIONAL STRUCTURE ON VIDEOTAPE: DYSFUNCTIONS LUCKY DIP

INTRODUCTION

A dysfunction arises in a family system which is organised so as to resist the change required by an outside event . If they are able to observe dysfunctions on tape, it offers course participants the feeling of reality around the idea of dysfunctions – they can see them! The labelling of dysfunctional sub-systems helps course participants to give new meanings to relationships they observe in the system. This is the first step towards the restructuring process.

Aim: Identification of dysfunction in the family system.

Task

1.   The teacher needs to prepare slips of paper with a dysfunction written on each one and put them into a hat or suitable receptacle. These dysfunctions should be ones the course participants might see on the videotape.

2.   Each person chooses a slip of paper from the lucky dip.

3.   The videotape can then be shown for about 10 minutes and the trainees can look for *their* dysfunction on the tape.

Closing the Exercise

General discussion. The group can be asked if they can name dysfunctional relationships in families they are working with.

Further Suggestions
The group can be asked to think of a family they are working with which shows a particular dysfunction and bring this back for discussion next time.

Reading
Minuchin, S. (1974) *Families and Family Therapy.* Tavistock: London.

Ratings
Preparation Time:

Minimum Time Necessary:

Level of Experience Needed:

Exercise 7:

RESTRUCTURING ROLE PLAY

INTRODUCTION

Restructuring is a general description of the technique of intervention used in structural family therapy; that is, the transformation of family structure so that the family can accommodate to
change without the dysfunctions that lead to symptoms in one
family member. Teaching restructuring through role play gives
meaning to theoretical ideas in structural change since course
participants have the opportunity to see it in action. This exercise
can have dramatic impact and may leave a considerable
aftermath that should be taken into account by the teacher.

Aim: Skills practice of restructuring techniques.

Task

1.   A member of the group can be asked to present a family
      they are currently working with.

2.   The teacher or presenter can draw the family tree on the
      board.

3.   The group can be divided into fours. One group can role
      play the family and the other groups can be teams of
      therapists.

4.   Whilst the family is planning their role play, the therapist
      groups are asked to map the family and to plan how each
      therapist might intervene to restructure the family.

5.   Each therapist is then offered the opportunity to interview
      the family for about 5 minutes. This time can be extended
      depending on the number of therapists. The therapists
      could work in pairs.

Closing the Exercise
General feedback and de-roling, paying particular attention to take appropriate feedback from all members of the family. The focus is on the effect of the therapist on the family structure and how this process occurs.

Further suggestions
1.   This is sometimes an intensive experience for the group because it involves change and it can be useful to videotape the role play for later review.

2.   Course participants could view a videotape of a structural therapist at work with a family. They could be given the structure of the family beforehand and asked to guess what re-structuring techniques might be used, perhaps role-playing it first and then viewing the videotape afterwards.

Reading
Minuchin, S. and Fishman, H.C. (1981) *Family Therapy Techniques*.
        Harvard University Press: London.
        Chapter 10.

Minuchin, S. (1974) *Families and Family Therapy*.
        Tavistock: London.
        Chapter 8.

Ratings
Preparation Time:

Minimum Time Necessary: ●

Level of Experience Needed: ✓

Exercise 8:

IDENTIFYING UNBALANCING TECHNIQUES FROM ROLE PLAY

INTRODUCTION

This exercise usefully follows a theoretical presentation of unbalancing. It will be important to make a distinction between boundary-making and unbalancing. In boundary-making, the intention is to change family sub-system membership, whereas in unbalancing, the intention is to change the hierarchical relationship of members of a sub-system. This exercise will usually demonstrate not only unbalancing but also the effect of unbalancing. This may uncover all kinds of possibilities within the sub-systems that people in the group may want to address. For example, in a parent child sub-system, if you change the hierarchical arrangements, it may leave other members of the family more or less vulnerable. This exercise introduces an element of fun and play useful for lightening the group's mood.

Aim: Skills practice of unbalancing techniques.

Task

1. The group can be divided into two to devise a therapeutic scenario to demonstrate one of the unbalancing techniques, for example creating affiliations or creating coalitions.

2. Each group can then play the scenario for the others who have to guess the therapeutic technique employed.

Closing the Exercise
No formal closing.

Further Suggestions
1.   If you wish to take this further, the group could look at videotape to look for unbalancing techniques.

2.   A course participant can be asked to present a case briefly and groups could each consider the effect of the unbalancing techniques on the family. These could be presented in turn in the large group and the presenter could comment on their usefulness.

Reading
Minuchin, S. and Fishman, H. C. (1981) *Family Therapy Techniques.* Harvard University Press: Cambridge, Mass.

Minuchin, S. (1974) *Familico and Family Thorapy.* Tavistock: London.

Ratings
Preparation Time: ✍

Minimum Time Necessary: ◔

Level of Experience Needed: ✓

Exercise 9:

PROMOTING ENACTMENT

INTRODUCTION

The task in this exercise is to help trainees to get a family to demonstrate how they relate to one another, in the context of the problem they have brought to therapy, usually as a prelude to suggesting different patterns of interaction which would be more functional to the family system. The demonstration from the teacher following a short theoretical presentation on enactment is a key component of this exercise since it enables course participants to make the link between theory and practice and experience the powerful effect of this technique. This is an exercise where people are able to intervene and see immediate results and it is therefore most encouraging for them.

Aim: Skills practice in promoting enactment.

Task

1.   The teacher selects two members of the group to be a mother and father. The parents are given a script, e.g., a couple who disagree on the way they discipline their teenage son.

2.   The teacher, together with a member of the group can act as therapist to promote an enactment between the parents, for example to ask the parents to demonstrate what happened when they asked their son to return home from a disco by 10 pm.

3.   The teacher can then underline the links between the earlier theoretical presentation of enactment and the role play example.

4.   The teacher can then ask the group to divide into threes, a therapist and two family members, and ask the group to repeat the exercise, using different family examples of their own. The teacher can mingle with the groups.

Closing the Exercise
No special closing tasks.

Further suggestions
This exercise could be incorporated into a full role play to encourage people to use enactments in the context of a full therapy session.

Reading

Minuchin, S. & Fishman, H. C. (1981) *Family Therapy Techniques.* Harvard University Press: Cambridge, Mass.

Satir, V. (1972) *Peoplemaking.* Science and Behaviour Books: Palo Alto, California.

Ratings
Preparation Time.

Minimum Time Necessary:

Level of Experience Needed: ✓

Exercise 10:

FOCUSING

INTRODUCTION

One of the most difficult tasks is for people to become process-orientated rather than content-orientated in their work with families. This exercise asks course participants to limit their area of enquiry to a small area of content and to explore it within the context of a restructuring or unbalancing plan. The therapist in this exercise may be quite proficient at the task. However, there needs to be an illustration of how easy it is to go off course and, in that case, you might ask the role playing therapist to "do it wrong".

Aim: Skills practice of focusing.

Task

1.   The group can be asked to briefly (5 minutes) present a family.

2   The teacher and the group can together draw a map of the family and make a re-structuring or unbalancing plan.

3.   The focus of the session is decided upon, i.e., the small area around which the therapist will question.

4.   The family members can be selected for role play. The observing group are the therapists and are asked, in turn, to interview the family. The therapists will continue to interview for three minutes or until such time as one of the observing therapists think that the therapist has gone beyond the limit of the focus decided upon earlier. At this time, the therapist can change over.

Closing the Exercise
A discussion about the effect of focusing on the structure of the family.

Further Suggestions
This could be developed in the context of a full role play or be part of a full role play. It could be done in small groups and could even be done in pairs with a therapist interviewing one other person.

Reading
Minuchin, S. and Fishman, H.C. (1981) *Family Therapy Techniques.*
       Harvard University Press: Cambridge, Mass.

Ratings
Preparation Time:

Minimum Time Necessary:

Level of Experience Needed:

Exercise 11:

PRACTISING INTENSIFICATION

Introduction

It is essential that this exercise is prefaced by an explanation of Minuchin's meaning of intensification by which he means amplifying or exaggerating a dysfunctional interaction as a challenge to the existing structure. There are a number of different methods that he describes, i.e., repetition of the message, repetition of isomorphic transactions, changing the time and resisting the family pull. These will need to be described beforehand and can all be practised within this exercise.

Aim: Skills practice of intensification.

Task

1.   The group can be asked to present a family.

2.   The group can be asked to map the family.

3.   The group can make a restructuring plan.

4.   The teacher can decide with the group what area to focus on for the interview.

5.   The group can then plan the interview with the instruction that the therapist will attempt to restructure the family with the use of intensification techniques.

6.   The role play can be set up and enacted. Everybody in the group needs to have a part in the role play in some form. It is helpful to have two therapists from the group working

together. Should the therapist find it difficult to stay on task, alternative therapists could be substituted during the role play.

Closing the Exercise
De-roling and feedback, emphasising the experience of the therapists in their attempts to make a difference. The temptation is frequently to reduce intensity rather than staying with the tension of the session.

Further suggestions
1. It is possible in this exercise that therapists do not succeed in the task and it may be necessary for the teacher to assist to ensure that both the trainees, therapist and the role play family experience some power in the technique.

2. If the group is too large for one family and two therapists, two families could role play side by side. This, however, has the disadvantage that it makes it difficult for the teacher to keep in touch with both of them.

3. This exercise could be amplified into a pairs exercise in which a subject could be nominated and one of the pair would interview the other using intensification techniques as a challenge to that structure.

4. A further simplification would be to select one or two intensification techniques only for role play.

Reading
Minuchin, S. and Fishman, H.C. (1981) *Family Therapy Techniques.* Harvard University Press: Cambridge, Mass.

Ratings
Preparation Time: ✐ ✐

Minimum Time Necessary:

Level of Experience Needed: ✓

Exercise 12:

COMPLEMENTARITY AS A SAVING GRACE

INTRODUCTION

When Minuchin talks about complementarity, he is particularly concerned about the battles that people get into within the family context. To illustrate this, he maintains that the therapist should be able to extend the family member's view of their behaviour to see not only one interaction but "the whole dance". This exercise is the first practice for participants to address disagreements between family members in such a way as to make them therapeutically useful.

Aim: Skills practice of complementarity.

Task

1.   The group can be divided into threes; two family members and a therapist.

2.   The two family members enact a disagreement and the task of the therapist is to intervene by expanding the context of the argument by, for example, including significant other family members in the questions.

Closing the Exercise

The group can be asked for the three most useful responses from the therapists.

Further Suggestions
This exercise could be done with a whole family role play.

Reading
Minuchin, S. and Fishman, H. C. (1981) *Family Therapy Techniques.*
Harvard University Press, Cambridge, Mass.

Ratings
Preparation Time:

Minimum Time Necessary:

Level of Experience Needed: ✓

Exercise 13

REFRAMING CRITICAL STATEMENTS

INTRODUCTION

Reframing refers to the therapist's attempt to provide alternative explanations for the family problem other than that offered by the family. These usually refer to the function of the symptom in maintaining homoeostasis in the system. People find reframing a difficult skill to learn and the feedback we have received over the years is that trainees would always like more time to fully understand it. There is very little written on how to practise what is such a central activity in all the approaches and we therefore give it priority in our teaching. It is possible to prepare reframe statements before the session, but it is preferable to ask course participants to reframe their own ideas as this avoids them being stuck with the teacher's solution and allows the teacher to help them to develop their own.

Aim: Skills practice of reframing.

Task

1.   The group of any size but equal numbers can be asked to give examples of critical statements they have heard families make about their problems. These can be written up on a board or flip- chart.

2.   Statements are then reframed in the large group as examples.

3.   The group is then asked to join in pairs and each is given one of the remaining statements to reframe. The instruction would be one of the following:

      (a)   Reframe your statement; or,

(b)   Produce three reframes of your statement, starting with the most outrageous reframe you can think of and then two more.

Closing the Exercise
The teacher can comment on the reframes. This can be used to develop teaching points, for example, negative connotation comes up frequently in trainees' reframes.

Further Suggestions
1.   To clarify this exercise, a person from the group or the teacher could be nominated to write reframe on the board. Additional reframes could be invited.

2.   As a development of this exercise, the teacher can attempt to reframe statements made during social conversation of the groups over coffee. For example, if someone said "I had a terrible time getting here", the teacher might say "It shows your commitment to the course that you made it!". The teacher can then encourage group members to join in with their own reframes of other comments.

Reading
Minuchin, S. and Fishman, H. C. (1981) *Family Therapy Techniques.* Harvard University Press: Cambridge, Mass.

Ratings
Preparation Time:

Minimum Time Necessary:

Level of Experience Needed: ✓ ✓ ✓ ✓

Chapter 5

Strategic Family Therapy:

TEACHING EXERCISES

STRATEGIC FAMILY THERAPY

Introduction

Strategic Family Therapy covers not a single model but incorporates a number of therapists who apply their ideas in different ways. These therapists have developed their own following and are sometimes regarded as belonging to different schools of practice. We have grouped them together theoretically and have chosen as examples Fisch, Weakland and Watzlawick at MRI; Steve de Shazer and Alex Molner at BFTC; Jay Haley; Chloe Madanes; Peggy Papp & Olga Silverstein respectively. We do not claim to do justice to these strategic therapists but include exercises which we hope are representative of each group.

STRATEGIC FAMILY THERAPY

Introduction

MRI (Brief Therapy Centre of the Mental Research Institute of Palo Alto)

INTRODUCTION

The work of this school has emerged from fifteen years of clinical research at the Brief Therapy Centre of the Mental Research Institute in Palo Alto. This work was originally stimulated by the innovative work of Milton Erikson.

MRI view problems as undesirable behaviour in the present. To be a problem, the behaviour must be performed repeatedly. Great importance is attached to the context of the problem and other behaviours. For a difficulty to turn into a problem two conditions need apply:

1.   The difficulty is mishandled; and,

2.   When the difficulty is not resolved, more of the same solution is applied.

MRI believe that, given this perspective, the therapist needs to become an active agent of change. Practising some of the techniques associated with MRI proves most helpful in developing a working therapeutic style. Exercises here will particularly address the practical application of concepts rather than the presentation of the theory itself.

Exercise 14:

THERAPIST MANOEUVRABILITY

INTRODUCTION

It is important to introduce this exercise by presenting the concept of therapist manoeuvrability as described by Fisch *et al.* (1982), that is that the therapist needs to be able to change his/her behaviour in relationship to the family as part of the therapeutic strategy in order to challenge the repetitive patterns of behaviour around the problem.

The teacher can present the areas of therapist manoeuvrability named by Fisch *et al.*:

(a)   Timing and pacing

(b)   Taking one's time

(c)   Use of qualifying language

(d)   Getting the client to be specific

(e)   One-downmanship

(f)   Individual and conjoint sessions

(g)   Tactics with difficult clients

This theory is usually easily understood by course participants and they can then make the connection to practice.

Aim: Skills practice of techniques of therapist manoeuvrability.

Task
1.   The teacher can choose an area of therapist manoeuvrability for exploration, for example, one-downmanship.

2.   The teacher can invite a case illustration from participants.

3.   Two course participants can be asked to role play the dialogue between client and therapist, attempting to use the technique selected.

4.   The teacher can help the therapist to use the technique by prompting him or her throughout.

Closing the Exercise
De-roling is not usually necessary here since conversations are likely to be brief and specific. This could close with feedback from the observing group but is usually more usefully extended by recommending continued practice in pairs by the whole group.

Further Suggestions
1.   The technique could be practised within a large role play and more than one could be explored at the same time. This is usually quite complex and our experience suggests simplification at all times.

2.   The group could be asked to work in pairs, each allocated a different technique of therapist manoeuvrability. A large group feedback would then complete the exercise.

Reading
Fisch, R. et al. (1982) The Tactics of Change. Jossey-Bass: London. Especially Chapter 2.

Ratings
Preparation Time: 🖊 🖊

Minimum Time Necessary: ◐

Level of Experience Needed: ✔ ✔ ✔ ✔

Exercise 15:

PATIENT POSITION

INTRODUCTION

This exercise challenges participants to engage the co-operation of the patient, crucial for the successful outcome of treatment. MRI contend that, if you are able to assess the position the patient takes, you will then be able to offer information that patients will probably accept. It will be important to the teacher to explain the concept and offer examples of how the therapist might act on his/her observations of patient position so as to facilitate change. This exercise is simple in design and addresses participants' temptation to confront or attempt to reason with clients.

Aim: Introduction to the concept of patient position and related skills.

Task

1.   The teacher can divide the group into two smaller groups.

2.   The teacher can ask each group to provide a case for illustration, preferably a new referral.

3.   Each group can be invited to assess the patient's position in relation to the therapist.

4.   Group 2 can then become the therapy team for Group 1 and vice versa. Various strategies can be practised in which a patient position is explored and challenged. The therapist team could decide to offer a task, an intervention or simply carry out an interview to enhance patient co-operation.

Closing the Exercise
De-roling would be necessary here. A brief overview of the teacher's observations about the interviews would be useful to connect the theory to the practice.

Further Suggestions
This exercise also addresses issues about therapist manoeuvrability. These could be noted and commented upon during the exercise for greater complexity.

Reading
Fisch, R., *et al.* (1982) *The Tactics of Change.* Jossey-Bass: London.
             Especially Chapter 5.

Ratings
Preparation Time:

Minimum Time Necessary:

Level of Experience Needed:

Exercise 16:

MRI STRATEGIC INTERVENTIONS - A HOST OF POSSIBILITIES

INTRODUCTION

The MRI describe their interventive techniques with extraordinary clarity which facilitates the task for teacher and course participants. There are, however, many different constructions and, to offer one exercise only would limit the options. This exercise is set as a general framework in which any of the interventions could be explored. It would be useful to provide a handout or write up on a board in point form the two categories of interventions (Fisch *et al.*, 1982).

MAJOR INTERVENTIONS AND GENERAL INTERVENTIONS AND THEIR COMPONENTS

A) Major Interventions

1. Attempting to force something that can occur spontaneously.

2. Attempting to master a feared event by postponing.

3. Attempting to reach accord by opposition.

4. Attempting to gain compliance through voluntarism.

5. Confirming the accuser's suspicions by defending oneself.

B) General Interventions

1. Go slow.

2. Pointing out the dangers of improvement.

3.   Making a U-turn.

4.   How to worsen the problem.

The objective is above all to expand the participants' creative thinking and then to help them to put ideas into a framework in line with patient position.

Participants find these difficult but most challenging and enjoy getting in touch with some crazy ideas and seeing if they can make any sense.

Aim: Skills practice of making strategic interventions.

Task
Theoretical presentation before the exercise will be presumed.

1.   The teacher can direct course participants' attention to the handout or written information about the two categories of interventions and go through these carefully, explaining each point.

2.   The teacher can ask trainees to divide into pairs, a therapist and a client.

3.   One of the pair could be asked to describe a problem (this could be personal or client-based).

4.   Each therapist is invited to identify the intervention type they wish to try.

5.   The therapist can then interview the client for 5–10 minutes.

6.   Once the therapist has sufficient information, the therapist can be instructed to take a break and write down a proposed intervention.

7.   When all therapists have an intervention ready, they are asked to deliver these and to end further interaction; this has the effect of intensifying the experience.

8.   A mood change in the group often follows the interventions. Confusion, challenge, laughter, resistance, etc. – a few moments may need to pass before some general

feedback from the group can be invited. The teacher could prepare particular questions for example, "Is this an intervention you might try again?" "How would you do it differently next time? Would the role-play client be able to identify the intervention type and would they as therapists be inclined to try it with a client?"

Closing the Exercise

The closure to this exercise is usually about how to integrate these ideas into clinical practice. It is recommended that an immediate homework task can be given, i.e., "Practise the intervention you have used today with a family with whom you are working. Write down the intervention verbatim to share at the next session".

Further Suggestions

1.   Presenting too many different types of interventions in one session has left course participants somewhat over-whelmed and often deskilled. It is preferable to ensure that each course participant gets hold of one "type" of inter-vention by being able to practise this in the session. The exercise could be repeated should participants want to explore another intervention type.

2.   It could be interesting to enlarge the therapeutic context by including more family members to practise with. This could also address the more advanced trainees' requirements.

Reading

Fisch, R., et al. (1982) *The Tactics of Change.* Jossey-Bass: London, Especially Chapter 7.

Ratings

Preparation Time: ✍ ✍

Minimum Time Necessary: ◕

Level of Experience Needed: ✓ ✓ ✓

BFTC (BRIEF FAMILY THERAPY CENTRE)

INTRODUCTION

Steve De Shazer, Director of the Brief Family Therapy Centre in Milwaukee, Wisconsin has developed an approach which represents a shift from the Brief Therapy model developed at MRI. While he recognises that it is useful to find out as much as possible about the interactional patterns around the problem,he now focuses on solutions to the problems rather than the problems themselves. This is called "Solution-Focussed Therapy". For De Shazer, where the problem is the client's depression, what is crucial is to focus on what the client is doing when he is less depressed, or the exception to the "rule" that the client believes he is always depressed and that this cannot change. It is these exceptions which can be used to construct solution behaviours, or indeed the exceptions themselves may be the solution and the clients may only need to do more of what they are already doing. He has developed a clear structure for a first interview with the aim of developing a series of solution tasks which follow from it (De Shazer, 1984, 1987).

Exercise 17:

SETTING TASKS

INTRODUCTION

Family therapy has used setting tasks for families as interventions in many forms. Helping trainees to experiment with
setting tasks is always well received. It is a challenge to be able
to set a task to fit the family dilemma. This exercise presents a
variety of solution-focused therapeutic tasks and interventions
described by Steve De Shazer and Alex Molnar which they
embed in a clear conceptual frame. What is more, they offer
guidelines for the interview which direct the therapist to the
most appropriate task. The teacher is referred to De Shazer and
Molnar for a full description. Participants gain important clinical
experience that is readily put into practice in their agencies.

Aim: Skills practice of solution–focused therapy.

Task

1.   The teacher can give a description of the De Shazer
      structure for a first interview (De Shazer, 1984, 1987) clearly
      labelling the three tasks, i.e., asking the family member to
      identify a solution or complaint statement which includes
      the treatment goal; to ask for exceptions to this answer, to
      then ask what is the difference in what happens when the
      problem is or is not present or to attempt to formulate
      potential exceptions.

2.   The group can be asked to divide into pairs, for one of the
      pair to nominate a problem (a non-serious problem from
      their own lives or a client problem) and for the partner to
      interview according to the three steps outlined.

3.   The teacher can prepare either on a flip chart or blackboard
      a representation of the flow chart presented by De Shazer
      and Molnar (1987) indicating the process of the interview
      that guides the final choice of task.

4. The teacher can read out to the group the list of the seven suggested interventions. Course participants can be asked to write them down (or a handout could be prepared) to have a "crib sheet" when practising selecting and delivering the task. The description of the interventions will need some clarification for course participants to be able to complete the exercise.

5. The original pairs are then asked to choose the most appropriate intervention for the problem presented.

Closing the Exercise
Each pair can be asked to read out their intervention and make some predictions for the future course of the therapy.

Further Suggestions
Depending on the time constraints, participants could repeat the exercise and select and give a task at the end. While tasks are being prepared, those participants awaiting a task can get together in pairs to guess the task they think they will be getting.

Reading
De Shazer, S. and Molnar, A. (1987) Solution-Focused Therapy: Toward the identification of therapeutic tasks. *Journal of Marital and Family Therapy*, 13, 4, pp. 345–358.

De Shazer, S. and Molnar, A. (1984) Four useful interventions in brief family therapy. *Journal of Marital and Family Therapy*, 10, 3.

Ratings
Preparation Time:

Minimum Time Necessary:

Level of Experience Needed: ✓ ✓ ✓

JAY HALEY

INTRODUCTION

Jay Haley's problem-solving approach is famous for the concept of "the solution is the problem". The ensuing rigid patterns of interaction become the focus of therapeutic intervention. These are explored in detail and the therapist by means of task-setting and reframing, seeks to encourage clients to perform different behaviours to the problem pattern. The therapist will also develop various strategic stances, for example expecting the problem person to become normal, in order to deal with the family's resistance to change.

Exercise 18:

MAKING A TRAINING TAPE "LEAVING HOME"

INTRODUCTION
This is a multi-level task in that the group is:

a)   presented core theory;

b)   asked to practise the theory; and,

c)   introduced to the use of audio-visual technology as part of practice.

Haley's work is well known to be teacher-friendly in that it is clearly presented and readily engages participants in putting it into practice. Taking into account that the leaving home transition is a fundamental life experience, it is this particular area of Haley's work that has been selected for an exercise. Experience has shown that these ideas have considerable impact, as participants are able to apply them to many other areas of their work. The teacher can present a handout which summarises Stages of Therapy, as follows:

(a)   The experts must organise themselves in such a way that one therapist takes responsibility for the case.

(b)   The therapist needs to gather the family for the first session and:

    1.   Focus on the problem person;

    2.   focus on what to do now;

    3.   Presume that the family hierarchy is in confusion;

    4.   Other conflicts in the family are ignored for the moment

5. Expect the problem person to become normal – do not excuse failure.

6. Expect the family to become unstable as the young person begins to become normal.

c) Therapy should be an intense engagement and rapid disengagement.

d) Occasional follow up to ensure positive changes.

Aim: Skills practice of Haley's styles of problem-solving therapy around theme of leaving home.

Task

1. The teacher needs to ensure the group is well in tune with the theory presented by Haley surrounding this topic. Reading could have been recommended; a group discussion; formal presentation, etc.

2. The teacher can then declare his/her position as producer of a Training Tape and ask for nominations for a director, a continuity announcer and appropriate technicians to ensure a fluent film.

3. The group can be asked for a family to role play that would fit the "Leaving Home" brief.

4. The teacher can present a handout/write up on the board the three stages of treatment nominated by Haley, expanding particularly on the issues that need to be clarified in Stage Two.

5. A role play can be prepared over a number of sessions to illustrate the various stages. It would not be necessary for the role play to be rehearsed before filming. It is helpful for the filming to occur as the role play develops. The continuity announcer will need to label each stage to be enacted. The producer with co-directors can assist the therapeutic process throughout.

Closing the Exercise
This is more usefully done on the next occasion that the group meets together. At this point, all levels of learning can be reviewed and both course participants and teacher have a tape that could be used in other contexts, e.g., course participants might wish to share this in their work places; the tape could be used for teaching purposes; the tape could be used for a teaching consultation for the teacher.

Further Suggestions
This task can be simplified by identifying only one area of the process described by Haley for practice and filming.

Reading
Haley, J. (1978) *Problem-Solving Therapy*. Jossey-Bass: San Franciso.

Haley, J. (1980) *Leaving Home*. McGraw-Hill: USA.

Ratings
Preparation Time:

Minimum Time Necessary:

Level of Experience Needed:

Exercise 19:

ORDEAL THERAPY

INTRODUCTION
This exercise has helped participants to expand their ideas about interventions, particularly setting tasks. Ordeal therapy refers to the attempt to set tasks which create more than, or an equal amount of stress produced by the symptom itself, thus addressing the losses and gains involved in maintaining the symptom. Participants enjoy the strategic rationale to the work and tend to try it out enthusiastically in the group. It is good fun and has a freeing effect on the thinking in the group.

Aim: Skills practice of ordeal therapy.

Task

PART 1
1.   Each alternate person in the group is nominated with the number one and asked to talk to the person on their left.

2.   Number one of the pair is then asked to invite a "personal" symptom from the person on their left, e.g., "I am too fat"; "I am worried about a friend"; an issue at work, etc.

3.   Number one is then asked to explore with questioning:

      (a) The consequences of getting over the problem;

      (b) What that person would like to be doing more of that the "symptom" prevents; and,

      (c) What does that person lose on account of the "symptom".

PART 2

4. Number ones are then asked to turn to the person on their right and devise a task – something that would have to be done that would create more than or an equal amount of stress produced by the symptom.

Closing the Exercise

Here it is most important to share as many interventions as possible. It will be necessary to keep in mind that some pairs might be uncomfortable about offering the feedback in the group and it is probably best to ask for voluntary reporting at random. This is a most enjoyable event for the group and the teacher since the feedback demonstrates the group's creativity.

Further Suggestions

If participants are sufficiently familiar with Haley's work, it might be possible to simply set the task and use the closing to review the theoretical rationale.

Reading

Haley J. (1984) *Ordeal Therapy.* Jossey-Bass: San Franciso.

Ratings

Preparation Time:

Minimum Time Necessary:

Level of Experience Needed:

CHLOE MADANES

INTRODUCTION
Chloe Madanes, co-founder of the Family Therapy Institute of Washington D.C. with Jay Haley, highlights seven elements which characterise her form of therapy.

1.   The therapist designs a strategy for managing each case.

2.   In order to change the interaction which surrounds the symptom, the therapist has to change the context of the interaction. This usually involves the family but could involve other systems, e.g., the school, other professionals.

3.   The directive is the main tool of the therapist. The directive can involve a small task given there and then, or a more lengthy one to be carried out at home.

4.   Optimism and hope characterise the therapist's stance in relation to the problem. Strategic therapists try numerous options until a workable strategy is found.

5.   The strategic therapist has strong respect for the client.

6.   The therapist is responsible for therapeutic change and does not blame the client for lack of progress. The therapist plans sessions, organises the problem-solving venture and is highly directive.

7.   Good strategic therapy is humorous.

Madanes has recently altered her thinking on therapeutic strategies in that, rather than designing a unique strategy for each case, she now lists and clarifies techniques she commonly uses but adapts for each case. She is particularly known for her work on marital problems and adolescence (with Jay Haley).

Exercise 20:

PRACTISING "PRETEND" AND OTHER TECHNIQUES

INTRODUCTION

"Pretend" refers to the therapist's request that a family member or family members pretend to have the symptom described. This challenges the notion that they are out of control of the problem behaviour and begins to loosen the connections in the rigid interaction pattern around the problem, leading to the possibility of new behaviours. We have selected only one of Madanes' techniques for this exercise, but have chosen a format that could be adapted to skills practice with a number of techniques. We think that as many as possible can be practised within the teaching session itself and that this is excellent material for homework practice. Participants value this work and like to spend time understanding and integrating this into their practice.

Aim: Skills practice of "pretend" technique.

Task
1.   One person can be asked to make a flippant complaint about some issue related to the training group, e.g., how uncomfortable the chair is, that the coffee is not tasty or that they are often cold in the room.

2.   The group is encouraged to respond to this complaint as productively as possible.

3.   The complainant is asked to continue.

4.   The complainant is then asked to pretend to have the complaint and the group is asked to respond as if the person was not pretending. This is rehearsed.

5.   The complainant is asked to leave the room and then return after a few minutes.

Closing the Exercise
The power of the paradox is experienced by the group and some discussion will be necessary to be able to leave that "symptom" behind. It is usual that the complainant finds it difficult to enact the problem since it is uncomfortable to receive the phony response from the group. This experience can then be linked back to the theory.

Further Suggestions
It is very powerful to continue to use the group context to illustrate other techniques, e.g.
(a) *Marital problems*
     Enact a couple in the group and engage the group in an attempt to challenge the incongruity in the relationship. The battle for power between two people is always an interesting issue to role play.
(b) *Adolescence*
     Putting parents in charge is easily played in the group with three participants trying to change the power hierarchy between them.
(c) *Finding the humorous alternative*
     This is a rich area for practice within the group and is readily played by participants. This could involve asking the group to either redefine a situation that would include an element of humour or to introduce "humorous" actions that could reorganise the context.

Of course, real case material can be used at all times if preferred.

Reading

Madanes, C. (1981) *Strategic Family Therapy*. Jossey-Bass: San Fransisco.
Madanes, C. (1980) Protection, paradox & pretending. *Family Process*, **19**. pp. 73–85.
Madanes, C. (1984) *Behind the One-Way Mirror.* Jossey-Bass: London.

Ratings
Preparation Time: ê ê ê

Minimum Time Necessary:

Level of Experience Needed: ✓ ✓ ✓

PEGGY PAPP and OLGA SILVERSTEIN

INTRODUCTION

A distinguishing feature of Papp and Silverstein's contribution to Brief Family Therapy is the use of a consultation group and team to assist in the dilemma of negotiating change. The group acts as a "Greek Chorus" in that it regularly sends in messages that provide a running commentary on the change process and the relationship between the family and the therapist. The group acts as a higher authority, like a "prophet" who sees into the future and predicts the consequences of change. Papp and Silverstein expand their ideas on the consultation team to a planned therapeutic debate which would include three therapists in the presence of the family, or "three-way debating". Their ideas for the consultation team are explained in the exercises which follow.

Exercise 21:

THE GREEK CHORUS – DEVISING SPLIT MESSAGES

INTRODUCTION

This exercise is best as the second part of a teaching session, where the first part would cover the theoretical rationale for change using these interventions. Trainees would be familiar with the notion of teams and their interaction with families. The split message refers to the delivery of a message which contains two opposing views. The family is thus challenged to integrate these to produce their own solution to their problem. The different types of split messages need to be defined before practice. If these ideas are not integrated into the systemic context of the family therapist whole, students often challenge them as unethical or manipulative. This practice though, is exciting for participants and their creativity can be given free rein.

Aim: Skills practice of devising and delivering split messages.

Task

1.   The teacher can ask for two presenting family problems from the group.

2.   The group can be asked to divide into two therapeutic teams to devise split messages for the "problem" that they would be most interested to try to change.

3.   When the interventions are ready, the leader of the team puts "his/her" team into the roles of the family (as many as she/he would choose); to place them in position, as if in the session – and deliver the message in role.

(It is important that this step be kept a surprise until the messages have been designed).

4.   Step 3 can be repeated with the second team.

Closing the Exercise
Feedback here is often self evident and "family members" share their immediate response. It is useful to ask family members not what it felt like, but rather "what do they think will happen before the next session?", i.e., future questions.

Further Suggestions
There are, of course, many different possibilities for practising designing split messages which participants can continue to practise. Practising in threes with two therapists and one family member simplifies the task and is outlined above. To complete the practice, it is fun to challenge people to practise in pairs in which each offers a "symptom" and each creates a split message as a member of a mythical team.

Reading
Papp, P. (1983) *The Process of Change*. Guilford Press. New York.

Ratings
Preparation Time: 📚 📚

Minimum Time Necessary: ◕

Level of Experience Needed: ✓ ✓ ✓

Exercise 22:

PRACTISING THREE-WAY DEBATING

INTRODUCTION

As in the previous exercise, it is presumed for this exercise that participants are familiar with the notion of therapeutic team work and in particular the use of split messages.

This technique is a development of split messages, in that it allows the consideration of further alternative views on the problem.

The task of debating is to share the family's dilemmas of change by articulating them out loud on their behalf. The different positions taken by the therapist push the family into selecting a position from which to evolve differently.

This exercise is usually enjoyed by participants who experience the effects of change directly.

Aim: Skills practice of three-way debating.

Task

1.   The teacher can ask for a volunteer to submit a dilemma for the group to work on. This is always best if it is one that belongs to the volunteer and preferably of nominal apparent significance, e.g. whether to buy a new washing machine or not; how to get the builders to complete the re-roofing of the house, etc.

2.   The group can be invited to interview the volunteer briefly.

3.   The group can be divided into three, asking each to nominate a position for the debate, i.e., two change positions, one no change position.

4.   Once each group has defined its position, they are asked to prepare their arguments for their positions.

5. Once they are ready, the three groups are encouraged to role play the debate to the presenter. The groups are instructed to remember to talk to each other, encouraging as many people as possible to make comments and to use any feedback from the "presenter" for their own argument.

6. The debate is left unresolved with each group reiterating their position.

Closing the Exercise
No further work is recommended. It is important that the teacher protect the "presenter" at all times and the teacher also needs to ensure that the arguments are balanced.

Further Suggestions:
The following exercise can be followed on immediately:
Course participants can be asked to divide into threes to nominate another dilemma and find three positions to debate. The trainer moves around to each group helping to develop the positions and encouraging the role play. This is an important follow-on as each participant is ensured a debating position with many having their own dilemmas debated. This is an exercise in exploring the consequences of change and being able to spell it out directly. Students value the openness of this task with families.

Reading
Papp, P. (1983) *The Process of Change.* Guilford Press: New York.

Simon, D.I. (1985) Dr. Boxford: A Mythical Consultant. *Journal of Family Therapy,* 7, 4, pp. 387–390.

Ratings
Preparation Time: 📖 📖

Minimum Time Necessary: ◕

Level of Experience Needed: ✓ ✓ ✓

Chapter 6

MILAN SYSTEMIC FAMILY THERAPY

Milan Systemic Family Therapy

INTRODUCTION

Milan Systemic Family Therapy is the approach drawing inspiration from the ideas of Bateson and Waltzlawick.

The approach is underpinned by the idea that change is brought about in family systems by the therapist interacting with the family in a way that introduces differences into the belief/behaviour pattern. When individual family members perceive sufficient differences, they will perceive a new context within which the problem behaviour and its accompanying beliefs acquire new meanings and are therefore, no longer seen as problems.

Some of the ideas that were developed in Campbell *et al.* (1988) have been developed further with our teaching groups and we present some of these here.

Exercise 23:

CONCEPTUALISING SYSTEMS: EXPERIENCING THE FAMILY AS A SYSTEM

INTRODUCTION

If course participants are to be able to develop an understanding of the theoretical ideas underpinning the Milan approach to family therapy and some skills in applying these in their own work, they will need to spend some time becoming familiar with systemic thinking. The Milan approach applies systemic thinking in specific ways in the therapeutic situation and looks to systemic thinkers in other fields of interest to provide it with new ideas which can be applied therapeutically, for example, Maturana from the field of biology (Maturana, 1978, 1980, 1988). This exercise allows people less familiar with family therapy to recognise the 'systemic' qualities of family life. Sequential discussion allows each person to change in response to the previous speaker. As this process continues, a systemic reality emerges.

Aim: Understanding the family as a system.

Task

1. The group is asked to offer an outline of a latest referral.

2. The group is divided into fours.

3. One person is nominated to begin by saying who they are in the family and how they have been responding to the problem. In sequence the next person nominates who he/she is, the effect of the problem on him/her and, in particular, the effect of the previous person's behaviour on him/her. If the constellation of the family is not clear, the group should be free to introduce fictitious characters.

4. Once each member has a position in relation to the next, the

group should continue to go round in sequence and begin their sentences with "if you continue to do that then I...".

5. After a little while, the trainer momentarily stops the discussion and introduces some new information. The teams are asked to continue their sequential discussion with this new information. The prospect of someone leaving is always a useful destabiliser, e.g., new job elsewhere, terminal illness, extra marital affair, etc.

Closing the Exercise
The group are asked to identify the theme that united their continuing discussion after the introduction of the new information. It is usually commonplace for trainees to be able to identify their panic from each of their positions in the system and their immediate attempts to prevent anyone leaving since the implication could be the break-up of the family unit. Some de-roling would be necessary as well as a description of systems and their resistance to change.

Further Suggestions
1. Participants could be set a homework task to try to identify some of the processes they experience in this exercise in families they are working with.
2. This exercise could lead into a more formal discussion on the characteristics of systems.

Reading
Bateson, G. (1973) *Steps to an Ecology of Mind*. Paladin: St.Albans.

Campbell, D., Draper, R. and Huffington, C. (1989) *Second Thoughts on the Theory and Practice of the Milan Approach to Family Therapy*. Karnac: London.

Palazzoli, M.S. *et al.* (1978) *Paradox and Counter Paradox*. Aronson: New York.

Ratings
Preparation Time:

Minimum Time Necessary:

Level of Experience Needed:

Exercise 24:

HYPOTHESISING ABOUT EACH OTHER

INTRODUCTION

It is important to make a distinction between a systemic hypothesis or formulation and a working hypothesis A systemic or overall hypothesis represents the therapist's point of view on the connection between beliefs, behaviour and relationships that he or she arrives at after working with the family. A working hypothesis is a tool which enables the therapist to interview the family and explore certain beliefs, behaviours and relationships which eventually lead on to an understanding of the meaning which the problem acquires in the wider system. As such, it is a set of ideas which stimulates the curiosity of the therapist and leads him or her to make connections between his or her own thinking and the feedback he or she receives from the family. We have found that course participants tend to confuse these two types of hypothesis and the effect of this is that they tend to hold on to their hypotheses as if they were the final answer or true in some way, rather than more or less useful. The focus of exercises around hypothesising is, therefore, on helping course participants to become better at generating new ideas for working hypotheses and to be ready to change them in response to feedback from the family.

The advantage of this exercise, leading on from a theoretical presentation about hypothesising, is that it allows people to see how to formalise their ideas or hunches about an issue into a hypothesis. The use of a here and now situation and each other makes this more immediate and less daunting.

Aim: Skills practice of hypothesising.

Task

1. The group can be divided into pairs and each person is asked to write down a hypothesis on "Why your partner has come on the course".

2. Each person then interviews the other for 5–10 minutes using their hypothesis.

3. Each then writes down "The hypothesis you think your partner had about you".

4. The pair can then share their hypotheses.

Closing the Exercise
General feedback.

Further Suggestions
This leads on to a family role play where the group constructs hypotheses around case material.

Reading
Campbell, D., Reder, P., Draper, R. and Pollard, D. (1983) *Working with the Milan Method: Twenty Questions*. Occasional Paper, Institute of Family Therapy: London.

Palazzoli M.S., *et al.* (1980) Hypothesizing—circularity— neutrality: Three guidelines for the conductor of the session. *Family Process*, 19, 1, pp. 3–12.

Ratings
Preparation Time:

Minimum Time Necessary:

Level of Experience Needed: ✓

Exercise 25:

DISCARDING HYPOTHESES

INTRODUCTION

We have found that course participants can become so attached to their hypotheses that they fail to appreciate contradictory feedback from families and they can then get stuck. The aim of this exercise is to help them to become more flexible in their thinking, being ready to adopt alternative hypotheses they have already prepared or in response to feedback from the family.

Aim: Skills practice of hypothesising.

Task

1. The group can be divided into fours and one of the group can be asked to briefly present a case for which they would like a new hypothesis.

2. The group is asked to come up with three possible hypotheses for the case and write them down.

3. The group is then asked to take the roles of therapist and three family members, with the case presenter taking the role of one of the family members.

4. An interview can then be role played for about 5–10 minutes, with the therapist using the first of three initial hypotheses.

5. The interview is then stopped and the therapist is asked to take a minute or two to develop a new hypothesis.The therapist can use either the second of the three initial hypotheses or another suggested by the feedback. In the latter case, the therapist should write this down.

6. A further 5–10 minutes of interviewing can follow.

7.   The interview is again stopped for the therapist to develop
      a further new hypothesis: this can be the third hypothesis
      or a new one. This should be written down. A last 5–10
      minutes of interviewing can follow.

Closing the Exercise
The small groups can review the process with the aim of coming
up with a further new hypothesis for future work. De-roling
should follow. The large group can then consider the whole
process; particularly looking at which of the hypotheses were
most useful, the initial ones as well as the feedback-generated
ideas, and how difficult or easy it was to discard them. The
trainees could be asked to characterise the therapist-family
relationship which developed and the teacher could develop this
into some input on the co-evolutionary process.

Further Suggestions
Course participants could be asked to record their changing
hypotheses by writing them down during their work with a
family in the following week, together with a statement
characterising the co-evolutionary process that developed.

Reading
Campbell, D., Reder, P., Draper, R. and Pollard, D. (1983) *Working
        with the Milan Method: Twenty Questions.* Occasional
        Paper, Institute of Family Therapy: London.

Cecchin, G. (1987) Hypothesizing, circularity and neutrality
        revisited: an invitation to curiosity. *Family Process,* **26,**
        pp. 405–413.

Ratings
Preparation Time: ✍

Minimum Time Necessary: ●

Level of Experience Needed: ✓ ✓ ✓ ✓

Exercise 26:

PLAYING WITH CIRCULAR QUESTIONING

INTRODUCTION

We notice from observing course participants that they often ask too many questions at the content level to fill the space so no new feedback is created and the sense of connectedness between the family and the therapist is lost. The course participant needs to be helped to stay connected to the family by remaining curious about them. We would think about asking course participants, "What questions can you ask which will keep you interested in the family?". The way the questions are framed are less important than the thinking which goes behind them. Various writers in the field have, however, categorised circular questions (Campbell *et al.*, 1983: Penn, 1982 and 1985; Tomm, 1985) and these writings form a valuable backdrop to our teaching.

Practising circular questioning is always a popular event as people are able to playfully experiment with colleagues. Initially the questioning is stilted whilst participants learn to take more risks and become less afraid to make mistakes. Linking one idea to the next is emphasised. Course participants respond quickly to lots of encouragement in this exercise.

Aim: Skills practice of circular questioning.

Task

1. The exercise needs to be prefaced by a theoretical introduction to circular questioning in which particular styles of questioning are defined.

2. The group is then divided into small groups (preferably pairs) and invited to study the Fleuridas paper (1986) – in particular to review the range of questions as a proposed "script" for practice (10 minutes).

3. The pairs are then asked to abandon their scripts, change their pairings and begin to interview each other using as many of the questions they would like to practise. No con-

tent is provided for the interview and is developed on an *ad hoc* basis by each pair. The teacher can visit each pair to help.

4.   Once the participants have had this first practice, two pairs are asked to join to form a team and each foursome is allocated a particular style of questioning, e.g., future questions, triadic questioning, etc.

5.   Each team in sequence is invited to question the teacher. The content is developed on an *ad hoc* basis. Each team is able to consult each other prior to asking the question to check its circularity and the thinking behind it. Each of the groups is encouraged to establish their hypotheses during the process.

Closing the exercise
When the teacher is questioned, the feedback to participants is powerful. The teacher is in a position to comment on the impact of the questions; which ones were challenging; which ones provoked self reflection etc. Participants are asked to share their experience of the questioning. The teacher needs to be careful not to go on too long since this exercise can be slow and needs to be followed by continued practice, perhaps a homework task, when the process is continuous and not artificially broken down as in this exercise.

Further Suggestions
Should the teacher be uncomfortable about being questioned, a family already known to the group or a family from a piece of tape can be used instead.

Reading
Fleuridas, C. *et al.* (1986) The evolution of circular questioning – training family therapists. *Journal of Marital and Family Therapy,* **12,** pp. 113–127.
Penn, P. (1982) Circular questioning. *Family Process,* **21,** 3, pp. 267–280
Penn, P. (1985) Feed-forward: future questions, future maps. *Family Process,* **24,** 3, pp. 299–310.

Ratings
Preparation Time:

Minimum Time Necessary:

Level of Experience Needed: ✓ ✓ ✓ ✓

Exercise 27:

IDENTIFYING CIRCULAR QUESTIONS FROM VIDEOTAPE

INTRODUCTION

Circular questioning can be a difficult skill to learn without some intensive skills practice. It is not a naturalistic style and often does not therefore come naturally to trainees. We think this is mainly because the Milan idea of information (what makes a difference) needs to be learned and integrated into course participants' practice. We find that course participants can "fall in love" with their hypotheses to such an extent that they lose touch with the feedback process. They become so keen on taking a family down a particular road, they are unable to appreciate from the feedback that the family is taking *them* somewhere. The process is not one of being several steps ahead of the family but of leading from one step behind, staying connected, and comparing their feedback with one's own point of view. It can be helpful for course participants to take part in an exercise like this where they focus on the feedback process. This allows them to see that they cannot do this without having a whole series of mini hypotheses which are changing all the time.

Aim: Identification of feedback process in circular questioning.

Task

1.   The teacher needs to have available a tape of a Milan Family Therapy interview, ideally one of the Milan associates at work.

2.   The teacher can give the course participants an outline of the family and presenting problem which they will see on the tape.

3.   They can then formulate their own hypotheses which can be shared in the group and then compared with those of the Milan therapists by watching the taped team discussion. This should take about 15 minutes so as the main emphasis of the exercise is the next step, as follows.

4.   The trainees can watch the taped interview for about 20

minutes, in 10 minute sections with a break in between and note:

(a)   Six good questions asked by the therapist and the family feedback which had triggered each question;

(b)   The family responses to these questions.

Closing the Exercise

General feedback with the particular emphasis of identifying what a "good" question is: Would the family agree? How did the responses change their hypotheses? What questions might they have asked given the same feedback from the family?, etc.

Further Suggestions

1.   The teacher could follow this up by briefly presenting different types of circular questions and then ask the group for a case and quickly set up a role play interview. The group members who are to act as therapists can then attempt to use some of the question types which have been seen on the tape or described by the teacher, e.g., classification questions, triadic questions, sub-system comparisons, etc. This could be concluded by a discussion on maintaining a balance between practising the questions and remaining sensitive to the feedback from the family.

2.   A role play interview could follow where the interviewer attempts to interview only by following the feedback. The interview could be stopped at "sticky points" so alternative questions can be suggested. The teacher can discuss the inevitability of having a hypothesis and the notion that there is no "right" question.

Reading

Penn, P. (1982) Circular questioning. *Family Process*, **21**, 3, pp. 267–280.

Penn, P. (1985) Feed-forward: future questions future maps. *Family Process*, **24**, 3, pp. 299–310.

Tomm, K. (1985) Circular interviewing; a multi-faceted clinical tool. In Campbell, D. and Draper, R. (Eds) *Applications of Systemic Family Therapy: The Milan Approach*. Grune and Stratton: London.

Ratings

Preparation Time:

Minimum Time Necessary:

Level of Experience Needed:

Exercise 28:

UNPACKING INTERVENTIONS

INTRODUCTION

It is important for course participants to appreciate that interventions are what happens when a family and a therapist are together; that is, that the whole interview can be seen as a punctuation in the family's experience which can make a difference to them. This is what is meant by: "interventive interviewing". This approach now puts less stress on the end-of-session intervention as the only way to make a difference to the family and this notion can be helpful to course participants who may have felt under pressure to come up with a powerful end-of-session intervention. We would now describe these interventions as giving feedback about the therapy team's experience during the interview.

It is important to make a distinction for course participants between making a formulation about the family system and thinking about what the therapist needs to do to create or facilitate a context for change in the form of an intervention.

It goes some way towards the over-emphasis on the "perfect" intervention to engage in an exercise in which interventions are unpacked and the family interaction reconstructed backwards on the basis of a final intervention. This is an "upside-down" method to the usual one of doing a role-play and then constructing various interventions. It has the virtue of novelty and allows course participants to attend to each part of an intervention in some detail in order to understand which aspect of family beliefs, actions or relationships it addresses.

Aim: Understanding of process of constructing interventions.

Task

1.   The teacher needs to spend some time beforehand selecting suitable interventions of various kinds, i.e., containing tasks and rituals as well as verbal messages.

2. The teacher can write up a selection of interventions on a board or flipchart.

3. The group is invited to discuss these, firstly from an aesthetic point of view – around length, type, format, use of positive connotation, etc., then leading into a more theoretical discussion on issues such as the Milan theory of change, first and second order change, difference between tasks in Milan family therapy and in other approaches.

4. Members of the group can then be asked to choose the intervention about which they are most curious and to group themselves in sixes. They are asked to construct a role-play family who might have been given this intervention; they are asked to take the roles of two family members, a therapy team of two and an observer team of two.

5. The groups are asked to think about the family and team issues which might have led to this particular intervention. Their discussion is to be focused around the following questions:

    (a) *For the family*
    1. What are your family beliefs/myths/assumptions?
    2. What do you think the therapist believes about you?
    3. How do you respond to the intervention?
    4. How do you give feedback about the effect of the intervention to the therapist?

    (b) *For the therapy team*
    1. What are the beliefs in the family you are trying to change?
    2. What is your belief about the family that led to the intervention?
    3. What do you hope might happen as a result of the intervention?
    4. What did happen?

    (c) *For the observers*
        What relationship do you observe between family beliefs and therapy team beliefs?

This should take about 10 minutes.

Further Suggestions

1.   Theoretical presentation of elements of an intervention, as a summary of the exercise.

2.   Videotape of a team discussion preparing an intervention, the intervention itself, the family response and following team discussion. The group could focus on what kind of family response might change their mind about the nature of the intervention offered.

3.   Videotape of a Milan team at work could be shown, say 10 minutes prior to the delivery of an intervention. The group could be divided into teams and each team asked to devise a particular kind of intervention, e.g., prescription, ritual or invariant prescription. The tape could be shown of the actual intervention given and a discussion could follow on the predicted effect of this, and of the intervention devised by the group on the family.

Reading

Campbell, D., Reder, P., Draper, R. and Pollard, D. (1983) *Working with the Milan Method: Twenty Questions*. Occasional Paper, Institute of Family Therapy: London.

Tomm, K. (1984a) One perspective on the Milan systemic approach: Part 1. Overview of development, theory and practice. *Journal of Marital and Family Therapy*, **10**, 2, pp. 113–125.

Tomm, K. (1984b) One perspective on the Milan systemic approach: Part 2. Description of session format, interviewing style and interventions. *Journal of Marital and Family Therapy*, **10**, 3, pp. 253–271.

Ratings

Preparation Time: 🖋 🖋

Minimum Time Necessary: ◗

Level of Experience Needed: ✓

Exercise 29:

MAKING NEUTRALITY ASSESSMENTS

INTRODUCTION

Neutrality has proved to be the most controversial and perhaps most misunderstood of the guidelines referred to in the "Hypothesizing – circularity – neutrality" paper published by the Milan team (Palazzoli *et al.*, 1980). Although their original definition referred to an attempt to conduct an interview so that each family member would feel the therapist had no favourites, the concept of neutrality has been applied to other contexts, such as the therapist's view of change. It has led to particular confusion in connection with cases in which the worker has a statutory role. In this connection, we would refer the reader to Campbell *et al.* (1989) pp. 37–45 for a detailed discussion of these issues together with case examples, which would be useful required reading for course participants embarking on a session on this topic. For the purposes of this introduction, we will define neutrality as a strategic stance arrived at by the therapist in a self-monitoring process. In that process, he or she is asking himself or herself what strategic stance needs to be taken in order to create the kind of relationship between himself or herself and the client which will bring about change. He or she is also thinking about how to create a situation in which this self-reflective process can also be conveyed to the client. This exercise allows participants to identify this process in the context of a role play family interview.

Aim: Understanding of the concept of neutrality.

Task
1.   The group can be asked to present a case briefly where they think that maintaining a neutral stance could be a difficulty.

2.   Members can be asked to take family roles, therapist plus

team of two and a group of observers.

3.   The family members can then prepare their roles and the therapy team can prepare a hypothesis. The therapy team and observers are asked to consider separately how they will attempt to maintain a neutral stance and to design some questions with this in mind.

4.   A role play interview of a first session can be enacted, including giving the family an intervention. This could be for about 40 minutes in total.

Closing the Exercise
The family members still in role, therapy team and observers are asked to join in the large group. They are asked to consider the following questions from their different perspectives:

For the therapy team and observers
(a)   Whose side was the therapist on?

(b)   If the therapist was on anybody's side how did this show?

(c)   What strategic stance could the therapist have taken?
(d)   Which questions would you like to have asked but stopped yourself?

For the family
(a)   Whose side was the therapist on?

(b)   If the therapist was on anybody's side, how did this show?

(c)   What strategic stance could the therapist have taken which might have helped you to feel the therapist was on your side?

Further Suggestions
This kind of exercise can be included in any role play on the Milan approach and it is useful to do this quite regularly so as to help trainees to appreciate neutrality in action as well as in theory. A homework task could be set for trainees to do a

"neutrality assessment" by answering the ending questions for themselves on families they are working with in their agencies.

Reading
Campbell, D., Draper, R. and Huffington, C. (1989) *Second Thoughts on the Theory and Practice of Milan Systemic Family Therapy.* Karnac: London.

Cecchin, G. (1988) Hypothesizing, circularity and neutrality revisited: An invitation to curiosity. *Family Process,* **27**, pp. 405–413.

Palazzoli, M.S., Boscolo, L., Cecchin, G. and Prata, G. (1980) Hypothesizing—circularity—neutrality; Three guidelines for the conductor of the session. *Family Process,* **19**, 1, pp. 3–12.

Ratings
Preparation Time: 🏍 🏍

Minimum Time Necessary: ⬤

Level of Experience Needed: ✓✓✓✓

Exercise 30:

POSITIVELY CONNOTING IRRITATIONS ABOUT FAMILIES

INTRODUCTION

The most common misunderstanding of this concept is to see it as a manipulative technique in which the therapist says something "bad", i.e., the symptomatic behaviour, is "good" in some way. Many course participants cannot tolerate the idea of "condoning" symptoms. They need to be able to appreciate that people do what they think is best or what they think they must do in order to prevent something that at the time seems worse from happening. The positive connotation is not of the symptomatic behaviour itself but of the intention behind it, of preserving relationships the way they are. Since the "problem" behaviour is observed from another context, that is, a "problem" context, it acquires a negative connotation.

It is important to distinguish between positive connotation as a strategy used as an intervention and a positive regard or appreciation of the beliefs and behaviours within the family which characterises the whole enquiry between the therapist and the family. It can be a helpful routine to get into the habit of positive connotation during hypothesising or at a stuck point in the session in order to develop more of a systemic perspective on the family. This exercise addresses this point.

Aim: Putting positive connotation into practice.

Task

1.   Members of the large group can be asked to volunteer some issues which irritate them about families they are working with. These can be written on a board or flipchart.

2.   The group can then be asked to think of positive connotations for each of these.

Closing the Exercise
General feedback with discussion of the implications of these positive connotations for the work with the family.

Further Suggestions
1.   A pairs exercise in which the pairs can share, "Who or what is most affected by you attending this session?". After about 10 minutes, each partner can try to produce a positive connotation for the other. This allows participants to appreciate the powerful effect of positive connotation for themselves.

2.   Videotape showing the use of positive connotation could be shown and the participants can look for instances and note them down.

3.   The teacher could make a distinction between the use of positive connotation as a characteristic of the interviewing style and as an element in an intervention. This could be practised in role play.

Reading
Campbell, D., Reder, P., Draper, R. and Pollard, D. (1983) *Working with the Milan Method: Twenty Questions.* Occasional Paper, No. 1, Institute of Family Therapy: London.

Campbell, D., Draper, R. and Huffington, C. (1989) *Second Thoughts on the Theory and Practice of the Milan Approach to Family Therapy.* Karnac: London.

Palazzoli, M.S., Boscolo, L., Cecchin, G. and Prata, G. (1978) *Paradox and Counter Paradox.* Aronson: New York.

Ratings
Preparation Time:

Minimum Time Necessary:

Level of Experience Needed: ✓✓✓✓

Exercise 31:

WHAT IS THE BIND?

INTRODUCTION

It can be a very useful way for trainees to understand some of the difficult theoretical ideas around double binds for them to get into the habit of being asked to think about the binds in a family member's position or for the family as a whole. They then find it easier to understand the dilemma or paradox the family presents to the therapist of "Change the symptom, but not the family" and the careful attention they will need to pay to the losses and gains around change for everyone in the family. When these ideas can be made real in this way, it is not so hard for trainees to grasp difficult writers like Bateson who are so fundamental to the development of this approach. Any family role play can be used for this exercise or it can take place as part of the therapy team activity with a real family in live supervision.

Aim: Understanding of the double bind in clinical practice.

Task

When the therapist stops for a break when stuck or to review a hypothesis, he or she can be asked, "What is the bind for x or y or for the whole family?" or indeed, "What is your therapeutic bind now?" This can be stated in the form, "What is it that x is damned if she does do and damned if she doesn't do?" For example in one group, a course member consulting to another member's agency dilemmas expressed the bind of a multi-disciplinary team in the following way: "This team has a dilemma about how to take decisions that affect its survival whilst holding on to the democratic ideal". At the stage of creating an intervention, these questions can form a basis of making a systemic formulation about the family. The bind can be written down by the therapy team and it can be a focus for the development of an intervention.

Closing the Exercise
At some stage the teacher must make a link with reading on the double bind.

Further Suggestions
Trainees can be asked to do this task in their agency work and bring feedback next time.

Reading
Bateson, G. (1973) Toward a theory of schizophrenia. In *Steps to an Ecology of Mind*. Paladin: St. Albans.

Palazzoli, M.S., Boscolo, L., Cecchin, G. and Prata, G. (1978) *Paradox and Counter-Paradox*. Aronson: New York.

Sluzki, C. and Ransom, D.C. (1976) *Double Bind: The Foundation of the Communicational Approach to the Family*. Grune and Stratton: New York.

Ratings
Preparation Time: ✍ ✍

Minimum Time Necessary: ◖

Level of Experience Needed: ✓✓✓✓

Exercise 32:

WORKING IN TEAMS: THE SEQUENTIAL DISCUSSION

INTRODUCTION

It is a fundamental aspect of the Milan Approach that therapists work in teams and it is important to give course participants the experience of team work on these courses. However, the reality for most course participants in their back home situation is that they work alone or at least with only one other colleague and often without video or screen. The risk is that they will say the Milan Approach has nothing to offer them because they cannot work in teams. It is, therefore, important to help them appreciate how systemic thinking can help them develop an internal dialogue or "team in your head" to help them articulate what they are looking for when working with families. This exercise can orient course participants to the possibilities of team work, specifically the development of a "team mind" and some ways to train the team. It is a common experience for the therapist to feel bombarded and confused by the ideas expressed by the team behind the screen when he/she takes a break for consultation or at the stage of developing an intervention. This exercise presents one way in which the therapist is enabled to organise his/her thoughts using the ideas of the team, whilst also developing an observer position on the therapeutic process.

Aim: Experience of the creation of a "team mind".

Task

1.   The group can be divided into eights and one person can be asked to briefly present a case for role play.

2.   The group can take the roles of four family members, therapist and team three.

3.   A role play interview can follow. When the therapist takes

a break, the team is asked to discuss their thoughts in the presence of the therapist, who remains silent. The team is asked to conduct their discussion separately, i.e., one person starts and then the next person who wishes to comment attempts to connect their ideas to the previous comment and so on. This can go on for 5–10 minutes, at which point the therapist can sit quietly to organise his/her thoughts and then resume the interview, or return to deliver an intervention to the family.

Closing the Exercise
De-roling and general feedback.

Further Suggestions
Other methods of team function can also be explored, e.g., that the team interviews the therapist, asking only one or two questions each.

Reading
Andersen, T. (1987) The reflecting team: Dialogue and meta-dialogue in clinical work. *Family Process*, 26, pp. 415–428.

Rabi, J. S. *et al.* (1984) The peer consultation team, an alternative. *Journal of Strategic and Systemic Therapies*, 3, pp. 66–71.

Whiffen, R. and Byng-Hall, J. (Eds.) (1982) *Family Therapy Supervision: Recent Developments in Practice.* Academic Press: London.

Ratings
Preparation Time: 🖉

Minimum Time Necessary: ●

Level of Experience Needed: ✔✔✔✔

Exercise 33:

CONSULTATION: CONSULTING TO EACH OTHER

INTRODUCTION

This is a classic exercise which always seems to be popular and effective in enabling the therapist to see him or herself as a part of a wider system which in turn affects his or her view about a particular family therapy case. We find that this taps a rich vein of systemic thinking which the therapist applies to his or her therapeutic relationship with the family. The interviewer gains equally from having to do a real "live" consultation. The participants are galvanised by having to make a real intervention and their learning is enhanced by the feedback they receive from this process.

Aim: Skills practice of consultation.

Task

1. In threes, each participant is asked to think about a problem he or she might have in working with families in his or her place of work.

2. Each person describes the conflicts or contradictions he or she experiences in trying to deal with this problem.

3. One person agrees to be interviewed by another and the third acts as an observer.

4. The interviewer for about 10 minutes should use circular questioning to:

    a) identify the patterns of behaviour that have developed around the conflicts.

    b) formulate ideas on how this pattern maintains important relationships and beliefs in their place of work.

    c) explore which behaviours of the interviewee maintain this pattern.

5.   After 10 minutes, the interviewer and observer make a hypothesis.

6.   After 10 minutes, the interviewer questions to explore the hypothesis.

7.   After 10 minutes, the interviewer and observer meet to prepare an intervention.

8.   The interviewer gives the intervention to the interviewee and lets the interviewee give some feedback.

Closing the Exercise
The threes are asked to discuss the process and to particularly address the question of what difference the consultation made to their thinking or, "What is the problem now?"

Further Suggestions
This exercise could lead into a theoretical presentation of second order cybernetics and how these ideas can be put into practice in the therapeutic process.

Reading

Campbell, D. (1985) The consultation interview. In Campbell, D. and Draper, R. (Eds) *Applications of Systemic Family Therapy: The Milan Approach*. Grune and Stratton: London, Ch. 19.

Lindsey, C. (1985) Consultation with professional and family systems in the context of residential and fostering services: In and out of care. In, Campbell, D. and Draper, R. (Eds) *Applications of Systemic Family Therapy: The Milan Approach*. Grune and Stratton: London, Ch. 22.

Ratings
Preparation Time:

Minimum Time Necessary: ●

Level of Experience Needed: ✓ ✓ ✓

Exercise 34:

THE REFERRING NETWORK

INTRODUCTION
Defining the professional network is regarded as a cornerstone in the development of the Milan Approach. The publication of the paper on the problem of the referring person (Palazzoli *et al.* 1980) had a dramatic impact on the field and course participants usually find these ideas extremely helpful. If they are unable to take on other ideas about the Milan Approach, for example the session format, teams, etc., they readily take on the idea of hypothesising around interacting systems, since so much of their practice involves dealing with families who are engaged with many helping agencies.

Aim: Exploration of thinking about the referring network around the family problem.

Task
1.   The teacher can present a letter of referral. This needs if possible to be a letter about a family involved with several agencies and the letter needs to give an indication of the relationship between the family and these agencies, especially the referrer.

2.   The group can be divided into twos or threes to work on the referral.

(a)   They can be asked to draw a network map, showing the family and the agencies with whom they are involved, indicating the connections between these agencies and their views of the problem.

(b)   They can hypothesise at two levels:
1)   About the family problem;
2)   About the problem of the referring person within the network of agencies involved.They can make notes about these and keep them (20 min).

3.   The whole group can then be asked to role play a referrals

meeting around this case. One member can be a team leader to chair the meeting. Five or six more can join the team to discuss the referral taking roles in an agency nominated by the team leader. The remaining members can observe the process, taking particular note of the extent to which hypotheses about the reframing network are taken into account in devising a plan of action.

4.   The team discussion about the referral can be played with the aim of coming up with a decision as to how the case should be handled, e.g., interview with family or part of family, telephone call to key person, network meeting, etc.

Closing the Exercise
Feedback from the observers to the team meeting about how referral network issues were incorporated. The teacher needs to highlight the options that were opened up via discussion of hypotheses about the network. It might be helpful to ask the group how they might have proceeded without this kind of discussion and what they would have to do in their agencies to enable such discussion to take place.

Further Suggestions
The group could be asked to undertake Step 2 with a referral they have in the next week for homework.

Reading
Dowling, E. and Osborne, E. (1985) *The Family and the School. A Joint Systems Approach to Problems with Children.* Routledge and Kegan Paul: London.

Palazzoli, M. S. *et al.* (1980) The problems of the referring person. *Journal of Marital and Family Therapy*, 6, 3–9.

Roberts, W. (1982). Preparation of the referral network: The professional and the family. In Bentovim, A. *et al.*, (Eds) *Family Therapy, Vol. 1*. Academic Press: London, pp. 159–171.

Ratings
Preparation Time:

Minimum Time Necessary:

Level of Experience Needed: ✓

Chapter 7

CONTRASTING THE MODELS

Contrasting the Models

INTRODUCTION

Since we have sometimes taught three discrete family therapy models, we have also developed ways for course participants to compare and contrast the models in order to facilitate their learning and help them to develop their own style. It is through exercises like this that people can move to an observer position in relation to the three models and then find the theoretical stance and relevant skills with which they feel comfortable.

Exercise 35:

CONTRASTING ASPECTS OF THE MODELS USING FAIRY TALES

INTRODUCTION
This is a enjoyable way of helping people integrate new ideas with ideas which are already familiar to most people. The power of the exercise is in using popular fairy tales as a common denominator to push course participants to make observations as if they were working therapeutically, but without the ethical restraint of working with real families.

Aim: Comparing and contrasting the ways the three family therapy models would approach the same case material.

Task

1.   The teacher can organise the group into teams to represent the family therapy models. Each team is asked to work according to a particular model.

2.   The groups can be asked to consider the following questions in relation to two or three fairy tales, e.g., *The Three Little Pigs, Red Riding Hood, Cinderella,* etc.

   a)   What is the problem behaviour?

   b)   What is maintaining it?

   c)   What intervention would you offer the family?

Closing the Exercise
Each team can feed back to the large group their answers to the questions. The teacher will need to draw out the differences and

similarities between the models, encouraging the particip-ants to do the same.

Further suggestions
1. This idea can be used at the beginning of a family therapy course, using different questions, to make observations of systemic patterns.

2. It would also be possible to work on one fairy tale and the exercise would then take less time.

Reading
Robinson, J. G. (1986) Fairy tales and teaching family therapy. *Journal of Family Therapy*, 8, 4, pp. 383–394.

Ratings
Preparation Time:

Minimum Time Necessary:

Level of Experience Needed: ✓ ✓ ✓ ✓

Exercise 36:

THE USE OF A FORMAL DEBATE

INTRODUCTION

Formal debating procedure is a format familiar to most course participants and teachers. It is a multi-level task in that it:

a. Requires the presentation (by at least four people) of coherent theoretical material, for example an exploration of the differences between Strategic and Milan family therapy. This is put in the form of a motion such as "This house believes that structural family therapy is a distinctive school and the others are both strategic", "This house believes that the three models can be used interchangeably to suit the therapist", or "This house believes that the three models are all systemic and need not be thought of as separate models of practice".

b. Requires that the audience are familiar with the theoretical material of the motion and come prepared with questions influenced by their own point of view.

c. Requires that participants take sides and that collaborative team efforts evolve.

d. Requires that the usual teaching/learning context is altered. The atmosphere of the group changes and provides a different context within which to learn. The teacher becomes a meta communicator to the content.

This is an interesting exercise. Participants usually take the motion very seriously and want to win. To do so depends on a coherent understanding of some key concepts since, in our experience, the audience is not very kind in that they present challenging questions with equal determination and clarity.

Aim: Clarifying theoretical similarities and differences
between the three family therapy models.

Task
1.   At least one week in advance, (preferably two) the group
can be told of the debating task and the motion is presented
to the group.

2.   The trainer invites:
(a)   a proposer for the motion;
(b)   a seconder for the motion;
(c)   a proposer against the motion;
(d)   a seconder against the motion;
(e)   a person to chair the debate.

3.   Each main player is asked to prepare a 5 minute presentation on their position.

4.   On the day of the debate, the chairperson is invited to lead
the day by inviting (a), (c), (b) and (d) (in that order) to
deliver their talks. The room should be formally prepared
with a top table and chairs facing.

5.   The remainder of the group are asked to divide into separate 'camps' depending on the motion to be debated and
each person is asked to prepare at least four questions to
ask from the floor.

6.   Once the motions have been formally presented and
seconded, the chairperson then opens the debate out to the
floor and invites questions from the audience.

7.   It is at this point, when discussion from the floor is completed, that a break for coffee is useful since the group is left
to buzz.

8.   The chairperson can then reconvene the meeting and (a)
and (c) are asked to sum up for each side.

9.   The vote is then taken.

Closing the Exercise

The chairperson ceremonially dismisses the meeting. No formal meta discussion is recommended. There is usually much mirth and teasing as people tend to continue to discuss their views.

Further Suggestions

1. A debate can be used not simply as a way of defining the differences between models, but for clarifying concepts within one model of practice only, e.g., debating the efficacy of the invariant prescription or debating gender issues relating to structural family therapy. Since it is a "dramatic" event in the life of the course, it is important that the motion chosen is one of universal interest to the group.

2. Group members can be asked to prepare "adverts" for each family therapy model to present to managers to advertise their practice. These can be visual or for radio or television. A further variation would be to design brochures for each approach. Some group participants could act as the managers to question those who have devised adverts and give feedback on their effectiveness.

Reading

Liddle, H. A. Analysis of six schools of thought. In Hanun, J. C. (Ed.) Keeney, B. P. (Vol. Ed.) *Diagnosis and Assessment in Family Therapy.* The Family Therapy Collector, Aspen Publications.

Liddle, H. A. (1982) On the problem of eclecticism; A call for epistemologic clarification and human-scale theories. *Family Process,* **21,** pp. 243–250.

Ratings

Preparation Time: ✍ ✍

Minimum Time Necessary: ● ◖

Level of Experience Needed: ✓ ✓ ✓ ✓

Exercise 37:

LEARNING TO
WORK DIFFERENTLY

INTRODUCTION
This is a risky exercise in that it depends for success on everyone having read the Gorell-Barnes and Campbell (1982) paper beforehand.

Aim: Clarifying the differences between structural and strategic family therapy but allowing group members to identify their own style of working and to experiment with a different one.

Task
1. The whole group can be invited to discuss the paper around the following questions:

    a) How did you understand the differences between the approaches at the level of
        1. Theory
        2. Practice
        3. The role of the therapist
        4. The role of the supervisor?

    b) How would you fit other approaches into this model?

    c) Which "side" do you identify with?

2. The group can then discuss more generally styles of working and each person can be asked to say what they would have to change to work differently.

3. A family can be presented by the teacher together with an initial hypothesis.

4. Group members are asked to role play the family and the remaining group members are asked to elect to be in one of two therapy teams, either structural or strategic. They are asked to choose to be in the team which will demand most of them in terms of changing their usual working style. They can be given about 15 minutes to prepare for the interview.

5. Each therapy team can then interview the family in turn for about 20 minutes.

Closing Exercise
General feedback in the large group together with consideration of possible end of session interventions from each of the therapy teams and the role play family speculating on the possible effects. De-roling for the family.

Reading
Gorell-Barnes, G. and Campbell, D. (1982) The impact of structural and strategic approaches on the supervision process: A supervisor is supervised. In Whiffen, R. and Byng-Hall, J. (Eds), *Family Therapy Supervision: Recent Developments in Practice*. Academic Press: London.

Stanton, M. D. (1981) An integrated structural/strategic approach to family therapy. *Journal of Marital and Family Therapy*, 7, pp. 427–439.

Ratings
Preparation Time: ✍ ✍

Minimum Time Necessary: ● ●

Level of Experience Needed: ✓ ✓ ✓ ✓

Exercise 38:

ASSESSMENT AND INTERVENTIONS FOR FAMILIES FROM THE "SOAPS"

INTRODUCTION

Almost all exercises and teaching at introductory level are based on material either from the participants' or from the teacher's experience. There is usually minimal opportunity to observe a real family and almost certainly no opportunity for these groups to operate as a team with a family equally familiar to all. Resorting to families of the media is one solution and introduces material which tends to engage everyone.

This is a reliable event to end a series of presentations of the models. Participants are offered the opportunity to test their thinking with colleagues who have different beliefs about the same family. It also offers an opportunity to define the same family according to three different models. The differences are highlighted through an experience in which course members are asked to think clinically about non-clinical experience.

Aim: Comparing and contrasting the ways the three family therapy models would approach non-clinical material.

Task

1.   Some weeks before presentation, ask the group which are their favourite soap operas, e.g., *Coronation Street*, *Dallas*, *Neighbours*. After the usual initial laughter and surprise, the teacher needs to explain that these soap operas will be the focus of exploration, using different family therapy models.

The teacher will need to encourage the group to choose two or three soap operas they enjoy so that participants can join together in two or three teams to work together for the exercise.

2.   Group participants can then be asked to watch their soap operas on the TV or radio in time for the event.

3.   On the day, the groups can be assembled and the attached form, or a similar one can be given to each team to complete (See Figure 1).

4.   During the exercise, the teacher can remain available to each team to help push them on to the next question.

Closing the Exercise
Feedback to this exercise has been taken in three ways:

a)   If the number of teams is small enough and time permits, each team can feed back their answers to the questions. This is excellent, since many of the other teams are also familiar with that family and the learning is increased.

b)   Feedback can be taken at a general level about the process of the exercise and meta communications about the task are invited, e.g., what were the most difficult questions for the team? Which were the most interesting? Which of the models are the more difficult to differentiate?, etc.

c)   No feedback is taken and the event (often not completed to the teams' satisfaction) becomes self explanatory. The teacher can prescribe continuing to observe or listen to the soaps to confirm or dispel the teams' formulations.

Further Suggestions
1.   If there are many "family" nominations, you might decide to complete this exercise in pairs with each pair addressing a different "family".

2.   This exercise can be done with no preparation beforehand provided enough people can join forces into teams who are familiar enough with a "soap".

3.   A number of variations on this is possible.

a)   You could nominate the group to watch a particular full-length film and work at it in a similar way.

b)   You could select a full-length feature film to show the group. This is done by showing a little each week and using the material to illustrate the particular notions. The continuity and group familiarity with 'this family' has considerable impact.

Reading
Bennun, I. (1986) Evaluating family therapy: a comparison of the Milan and problem solving approaches. *Journal of Family Therapy*, 8, 3, pp. 235–242.

Israelstam, K. (1988) Contrasting four major family therapy paradigms; implications for family therapy training. *Journal of Family Therapy*, 10, 2, pp. 179–196.

Ratings
Preparation Time: ✍

Minimum Time Necessary: ●

Level of Experience Needed: ✓✓✓✓

QUESTIONNAIRE ON THE "SOAPS"

1.   Map the family system within the wider network.

2.   Describe a problem which could be presented for family therapy.

3.   Who in the system might present this problem for family therapy and why?

4.   How might this problem have got to you? (State what agency you are.)

5.   Who has most to lose if the presenting problem is no longer there?

6.   Devise a hypothesis that will explain the function of the problem for each member of the system.

7.   Who might you invite to the first session?

8.   Devise at least 5 questions you might use to begin to explore your hypothesis.

9.   Imagine that your hypothesis has been confirmed,

   (a)   As if you were "Minuchin clones" write down what you would tell the family at the end of your session.

   (b)   As if you were the team practising with Boscolo and Cecchin, could you write down your intervention you offer to the family.

   (c)   You are a strategic team and have devised a strategic intervention to address the symptom. What was your intervention and what did you ask them to do?

10.   Imagine

   a)   A first order change in the system, and,

   b)   A second order change in the system. What would they be?

11.   Imagine the disappearance of the original "presenting problem", what new problem could take its place to keep the system essentially the same?

12.   Thinking systemically, how would you explain the appeal of a "soap opera"? What is its relationship to change?

Exercise 39:

NEW EPISTEMOLOGIES — CONSTRUCTIVISM

INTRODUCTION

The eighties have brought challenges to the philosophical and ethical foundations of family therapy practice. One of the most influential of these challenges is the writing on constructivism; the notion that individuals construct their own sense of reality and time (Von Glaserfeld, 1984). These basic constructs determine what behaviour is acceptable in order to maintain a comfortable ecology of ideas and behaviour. When new ideas intrude, family members may label certain differences between new and old behaviour as problems because important relationships may be threatened by them. Family members who observe and describe problem behaviour become part of a problem-determined system (Anderson *et al.*, 1987) of beliefs and their accompanying behaviours aimed at solving the problem.

What follows from these constructivist ideas is that therapeutic efforts are then not only directed at solving these "problems" directly, but at exploring the relationships in the system which may be connected to the problem-determined pattern. We believe it important for course participants at all levels to be introduced and encouraged to consider these challenges to basic assumptions both for their own curiosity as agents of change and for the development of a coherent body of practice. It is useful to introduce new epistemologies to participants well into the course as course participants can be left questioning their own beliefs, some just newly acquired. This can be experienced as too confusing and de-skilling early on, but stimulating and a real challenge to new learning later on.

Aim: Introducing the challenge of constructivism to family therapy theory and practice.

Task

1.   The teacher can select significant reading for the group to prepare in advance. (See Reading for suggestions.)

2.   The teacher can invite two volunteers to:

   a)   either be interviewed by the group, or,

   b)   to interview the teacher on constructivism and its application to clinical practice.

The exercise could end here but;

3.   A member of the group could then be asked to present a case briefly.

4.   The group can then be divided into fours and fives to work on the case. Taking into account the ideas they have heard about constructivism they can be asked to:

   a)   Devise a hypothesis;

   b)   Name their therapeutic objectives with this family and what they might do to get there;

   c)   Decide what some of the consequences of the proposed changes could be.

Closing the Exercise
This is most important since you wish to encourage the emergence of different realities about the same family and put these into the context of constructivist thinking.

Further Suggestions
The selection of constructivism as a different epistemological view is selected at random for illustration only.
   Other examples could be covered, for example, Erikson, De Shazer and White.

Reading
Anderson, H., Goolishian, H. and Windermand L. (1987) Problem-determined systems: towards transformation

in family therapy. *Journal of Strategic and Systemic Therapies*, 5, 4, pp.1–13.

Von Glaserfeld, E. (1984) An introduction to radical constructivism. In Watzlawick, P. (Ed), *The Invented Reality*. W.W. Norton: New York.

The Family Therapy Networker: *The Constructivist Challenge*. September/October 1988.

Ratings

Preparation Time: ✍ ✍

Minimum Time Necessary: ◕

Level of Experience Needed: ✓ ✓ ✓ ✓

Chapter 8

OTHER USEFUL EXERCISES

Other Useful Exercises

INTRODUCTION

Here we present four exercises which cover important aspects of family therapy teaching not covered by the previous headings. The first two, which directly address race and gender, deal with themes which should, in our opinion, run through all current family therapy practice. The third deals with how to integrate research initiatives with clinical practice; and the fourth presents a format for a live family therapy session taking place outside the context of live supervised practice.

Exercise 40:

MULTI-CULTURAL PRACTICE

INTRODUCTION

Issues connected with working with families of a mixed culture or culture different from that of the therapist team need to be constantly addressed throughout a family therapy training course to avoid therapists working with assumptions about family functioning which derive from only the cultural perspective of the therapist. This exercise could be simplified using only one or two steps of the exercise or could be divided into several teaching events. The impact on participants' clinical practice is always significant.

Aim: Introducing exploration of cultural perspectives into family therapy practice.

Task

1.   Theoretical input could be presented that could cover some of the following:

(a)   Consideration of assumptions we bring to therapy and the differences between an assumption and a hypothesis.

(b)   Noting the importance of viewing the meaning of symptoms within a particular culture.

(c)   Examples of potentially handicapping assumptions we may bring to work with families from cultures other than our own.

Examples

1.   O   A family from a particular culture will do better with a therapist from their own culture.

O   Afro-Carribean one parent families are deprived without regular presence of a father.

O   Asian children are diligent and hard working in school and their parents have high expectations of their achievement.

O   We need members of other cultures in *this* group so as to explore cross-cultural issues.

2.   The group is invited to list more of these from their own experience.

3.   A possible end to the exercise could be to divide the group into teams and to ask them to prepare a case for presentation to the other teams in which there is a challenging cultural issue. The presentation could take any form, e.g., role-play; setting the other groups an exercise; discussion; interview, etc.

4.   Each presentation should not take longer than 10 minutes.

Closing the Exercise
Since the event would already have taken the form of careful theoretical discussion it is important that the closing statements from the trainer connect the dilemmas presented with their clinical implications.

Further Suggestions
1.   A homework task could be offered, e.g., to bring agency equal opportunities policies and discuss in the session how these relate to clinical practice.

2.   Cultural issues can be addressed within tasks that relate to other conceptual material, e.g., structural interventions with families where hierarchies are culturally defined.

Reading
Barot, R. (1988) Social anthropology, ethnicity and family therapy. *Journal of Family Therapy*, **10**, pp. 271–282.

Lau, A. (1984) Transcultural issues in family therapy. *Journal of Family Therapy*, **6**, pp. 91–112.

McGoldrick, M., Pearce, J. K. and Giordano, J., Eds (1982) *Ethnicity and Family Therapy*. Guilford Press: New York.

Rating
Preparation Time:

Minimum Time Necessary:

Level of Experience Needed: ✓ ✓ ✓ ✓

Exercise 41:

A GENDER GAME

INTRODUCTION
Feminist challenges to current family therapy practice, especially around the area of child sexual abuse, need to be addressed directly in family therapy teaching. This exercise allows course participants to develop their consciousness of gender issues and see how this will affect clinical practice.

Aim: Introducing the exploration of gender assumptions into family therapy practice.

Task

1. The trainer can prepare at least five particular issues for discussion prior to the "game", for example a discussion of the five guidelines named by Walters *et al.* (1988) for family therapy from a feminist perspective:

    (a) Recognising patriarchal assumptions.

    (b) Identification of the gender message and social constructs that condition behaviour and sex roles.

    (d) Awareness of patterns that split the women in families as they seek to acquire power through relationship with men.

    (e) Recognising the basic principle that no intervention is gender free and that every intervention will have a different and special meaning for each sex.

2. A case can then be presented where gender issues seem predominant.

3. *The game*

    (a) The course participants can begin to role play the family.

    (b) Each observing participant in turn is expected to ask the family up to three questions of any kind, but without repetition, deviation or hesitation.

Hesitation =   apparent uncertainty as to whom to direct the question or how to word it to ensure "gender" neutrality.

Deviation =   avoiding a gender issue.

Repetition =   making the same mistake that has already been made by other interviewers.

(c)   The observing group is asked to shout out their challenge. The teacher, acting as chairperson, to the game, makes the final judgement and, if the challenge is agreed, the questioning goes to the next person.

(d)   Once correctly challenged, that interviewer is out and cannot ask any more questions. The task continues until there is only one person left. The objective is to see if there can be "a winner".

Closing the Exercise
A discussion of gender in the therapeutic context is useful to address the question of whether you can still work given the clinical issues that gender raises.

Further Suggestions
Participants can be asked to bring back a number (minimum two) of observations from their clinical practice where gender had an impact on a conversation or an event.

Reading
Goldner, V. (1988) Generation and gender: Normative and covert hierarchies. *Family Process*, **27**, pp. 17–31.

Walters, M. *et al.*, (1988) *The Invisible Web. Gender Patterns in Family Relationships.* The Guilford Press: New York.

Ratings
Preparation Time:

Minimum Time Necessary:

Level of Experience Needed: ✓ ✓ ✓ ✓

Exercise 42:

GENERATING IDEAS FOR RESEARCH AND PROJECTS FOR COURSE PARTICIPANTS AND TEACHERS.

INTRODUCTION

At the initial stages of absorbing new ideas, the prospect of putting these to the test in the form of projects for research seems remote. As participants develop their thinking and begin to integrate new ideas into their practice, we like to introduce the notion of research as a way of promoting their continuing development. This is a simple exercise that we hope encourages trainees to question their beliefs about their own practice.

Aim: Introducing methods of developing research in family therapy practice.

Task

1.   Before any theoretical ideas related to research as a science in itself are shared, the group is asked to nominate some of their favourite tasks in their clinical practice.

2.   One participant's topic is selected for exploration through questioning led by the teacher, who encourages continuing questioning from the group.

Examples – Historical questions:
1.   Where did you first learn about this topic?
2.   When did you first try these ideas?
3.   How have they changed since you first began to use the ideas?

Present questions
4.   What is the extent of the effect of ideas in your present practice?

5. Who else knows about this idea of yours?
6. Who else do you think might be interested in what you are doing?
7. Is anyone that you know doing the same thing or things?

Future questions
8. What would you have to do to be able to present what you are doing to your management?
9. How could you measure your effectiveness as a way of presenting your ideas?
10. What do you think you would have to change for this to become a task for more people to practise?

3. It does not take too long before the group becomes engaged in discussion of a project that could well become research.

Closing the Exercise
The discussion itself is often an intervention for others to begin to develop some of their own ideas in a different way. This exercise could be followed by some theoretical input from the teacher on how to shape their ideas into a piece of research or project.

Further Suggestions
The group could be given a simple task towards a research project for the group as a whole, e.g., designing an outline for writing up family sessions. Each participant could bring particular views and dilemmas from their own agencies and together compile data on different methods of writing up family work. A date for final completion of this work could be established and possible plans for publication and wider sharing of the ideas could be made.

Reading
Gorell-Barnes, G. (1982) Pattern and intervention: research findings and the development of family therapy theory. In Bentovim, A. *et al.*, (Eds) *Family Therapy*, Vol.1. Academic Press: London, pp. 131–155.

Ratings
Preparation Time:

Minimum Time Necessary: ●

Level of Experience Needed: ✓ ✓ ✓

Exercise 43:

OBSERVING A LIVE FAMILY SESSION

INTRODUCTION

Observation of a live family within the context of an introductory family therapy course which does not include live supervision is an invaluable learning experience for groups new to systemic practice. Many issues arise during the preparation, execution and the aftermath of the session that need to be carefully managed for the event to be successful.

Early in the course, the group can be asked to bear in mind the possibility of bringing a family with whom they are working for consultation. Should an offer occur, it could have a space on the course at any time during the year. It is important that the course participant bringing the case remains the therapist with clinical responsibility. The teacher can act as consultant, with other course participants observing the session. Their task needs to be firmly framed as an observation task. If this is not done and course participants attempt to contribute directly to the therapeutic process, the danger is of flooding the therapist with ideas and giving the teacher the double task of teacher to the group and consultant to the therapist. In our experience, it works best if the teacher acts primarily as consultant in this task and the consultation to the course participant/therapist is at the forefront.

Inviting a live family for observation raises a number of uncomfortable ethical issues that need to be addressed prior to the event. Special care needs to be given to the course participant bringing the family, appropriate networking between the agency and the course, the consultation contract between the therapist and teacher and the training needs of the group. This is a complex task requiring considerable preparation and skill from the teacher.

Aim: Developing observation skills in a live family therapy session.

Task

1. Once an offer of a family has been made by a course part-
    icipant, the teacher needs to address the initial preparation
    within the group, particularly the framing of the task also
    needs to be available to the course participant in the event
    of necessary further discussion.

2. Appropriate accommodation arrangements are necessary,
    e.g., viewing room and audio-visual equipment.

3. Careful preparation of the session is negotiated with the
    therapist particularly focusing on the aim of the consul-
    tation for the therapeutic task. It will be important for the
    teacher to be clear about what the therapist would like to
    achieve by the end of the session so he/she can ensure this
    happens.

4. The group are offered observation tasks in relation to the
    family or other material that is pertinent to the course at
    that time, e.g., gender or cultural issues. Careful attention
    should be given to devising a format for these tasks as well
    as how positive feedback will be given to the therapist, e.g.,
    "name three questions the therapist asked which made a
    difference", "describe the non-verbal behaviour of the
    family" to avoid the observers criticising the previous
    therapeutic work and the consultation task.

Closing the Exercise
Since time will no doubt be too short, discussion will continue
well into the next session. Whilst theoretical issues can be carefully addressed, it remains important to protect the therapist
from criticism and to give him/her ideas which will enable him/
her to move on more effectively with the family.

Further Suggestions
The participant bringing the family could be encouraged to
invite other people with whom they are working, e.g., students,
professionals from other agencies connected with the family, e.g.,
education welfare officer or even their manager. This broadens
the context and allows discussion of the management of change
in the interacting systems in which family therapy takes place.

Reading

Campbell, D. (1985) The consultation interview. In Campbell, D. and Draper, R. (Eds) *Applications of Systemic Family Therapy: The Milan Approach*. Grune and Stratton: London, pp. 193–202.

Whiffen, R. and Byng-Hall, J. (1982) *Family Therapy Supervision*. Academic Press: London.

Ratings

Preparation Time: 🖋 🖋 🖋

Minimum Time Necessary: ⬤ ⬤

Level of Experience Needed: ✓ ✓ ✓ ✓

Chapter 9

HOMEWORK
AND
COURSE PROJECTS

HOMEWORK
AND
COURSE PROJECTS

INTRODUCTION

Homework tasks provide a framework for trainees to apply new learning in their agency contexts. It is a constant struggle to ensure that the course sustains its relevance to participants' work practice and people are able to use new conceptual thinking in their work lives. The family therapy courses are usually part-time and it is difficult to make two hours a week during the academic year have a significant impact on a full working life. In our experience, the performance of homework tasks and course projects can become the cutting edge of the teaching–learning-experience and, as such, valuable feedback for the teacher on the effects of his/her efforts. When homework is not completed, the teacher needs to be alert to whether the task represented a "poor" homework task and to develop hypotheses as to why this should be, e.g., was it a task better set at a later stage in the course when trainees have a clearer understanding of a certain concept; were agency problems not sufficiently addressed beforehand and would consultation on agency issues be appropriate at this point? If successfully completed by some and not by others, do some individuals need to be offered individual sessions to discuss their problems about the task? In any case, the feedback from homework tasks and course projects is part of the valuable information you need as a teacher to plan the next stage of the learning. Sometimes, especially for individual tasks, it may not be important to take formal feedback on the results of the homework, but, in the case of pairs or small group work, it will be important to find a way of collecting formal feedback on the effects of the task. This could take the form of asking how it will shape future practice rather than going over what actually happened, which will emphasise redundancies in the agency or individual practice: If this is not done, it can sap the confidence of trainees who have tried hard to complete the task, sometimes with difficulty and perhaps miss the opportunity for further learning for all (e.g., how others managed to complete the task in their different agencies).

The difference between homework tasks and course projects is that homework tasks are usually set between sessions whereas projects are set over longer periods, for example holidays. We hope that this offers the opportunity for trainees to consolidate and explore their learning at a different pace and without the support of regular teaching sessions. We usually encourage people to link together to complete the tasks especially if they come from the same agency and are often surprised by the creativity this unleashes. We usually find that, far from wanting a rest in the holidays, course participants are eager to find ways to continue their learning and value a suggested structure for doing this. It is important to set projects which connect with the preoccupations of the group at that particular time so as to be able to link the feedback with further teaching.

We list a number of examples of homework tasks and course projects below, indicating how feedback can be built into the next session.

Homework Tasks

A – Skills Practice

1. Try out one idea you have heard today about interventions with a family or colleague and bring us the feedback next time.

2. Bring in your favourite intervention you have used with a family.

3. Try to change people's positions during a session, (Structural Family Therapy skill).

4. Try to ask future questions of a family, (Milan Family Therapy skill).

5. Try to practise the one-down position with a client, (Strategic Family Therapy skill).

6. Observe the questions you ask families in your agency next week. Bring one question you asked that you thought made a difference.

7. Every time a referrer mentions a problem to you in the next

week, do three reframes for yourself, the most outrageous first and then two more.

8.   Bring a case for which you think you need a hypothesis and make a hypothesis about why you think you have chosen this case.

9.   Make a geneogram of your own family/your agency.

10. Ask a family you are seeing to draw a picture of themselves doing something together; write a paragraph about what you think this indicates about family relationships and bring it next time.

11. Complete a profile of your self as a family therapist in your agency. This will require the preparation of a series of printed questions for course participants to answer, for example, "List four of your characteristics as a practitioner", "What are your strengths and weaknesses". "How would you describe your theory of change", "What will you have to give up to learn something new?" and many more. The purpose is for professional definition and future self evaluation. It can be reviewed at various points later in the course and could be the basis of individual tutorial sessions.

12. Ask course participants to write up a case in a framework suggested by you and bring it into the next session.

B – Reading
13. The teacher can ask course participants to read a paper for the next session:

   (a) The whole group can be asked to read the same paper;

   (b) Pairs can read the same paper;

   (c) Half the group can read one paper and the other half can read a paper presenting an opposing theoretical position;

(d)   People can choose chapters from a book on a particular theme;

(e)   Two people can be asked to take opposing views to present about a paper;

(f)   Pairs can be asked to re-read a paper from earlier in the course and together present a 5 minute presentation on the paper next time.

14.   The group can be organised in twos or threes to read skills papers or chapters, e.g., chapters in Minuchin and Fishman and ask them to be ready next time to demonstrate their skill in a role play.

15.   The group can be asked to choose an article from a current family therapy journal that arouses their curiosity. They can be asked to prepare a 5 minute presentation in which they:

(a)   Say where the article came from – the nature of the journal (spread of subject matter, style, expected readership);

(b)   Say something about the article to arouse the curiosity of others in the group;

(c)   Say whether they would put it on the course reading list for next term.

For those who did not manage the task, you could ask "What article do you wish you had written and to which journal would you submit it?"

16.   Ask course participants to prepare the necessary reading to take part in a debate on the 3 main approaches to family therapy; or a debate on any other issues, e.g., the systems approach to family therapy denies power and gender issues in families.

C – Consolidation of Theory

17.   Bring an example of metaphor used by a family and how you took it up.

18.   Bring case material on a family which involved some of the cultural issues you have heard about today.

19.   Write some notes about a case you are involved in in terms of concepts of the family life cycle.

20.   Write a page on a case which shows your understanding of the interacting systems in which the family is involved.

21.   Write a page on a case in terms of issues of gender.

D – Sharing Agency Practice
22.   Ask course participants to bring offerings from their agency work, e.g., videotape, case histories, printed publicity about agencies, video consent forms, agency practice about what is kept in files, equal opportunities policies, recording formats, etc. This can form valuable material for discussion on these issues in the next session.

23.   Course participants can be asked to try to visit each other in their agencies.

E – Evaluation of own Learning
24.   After you leave this first session, write down the four most important things you want to learn this term. You may want to consult your colleagues at work about this. Before you come next time, review this list and note any changes you would like to make in this list and hand it in with any amendments.

25.   Prepare a paragraph on the theory of change you use in working with families.

Course Projects

1. Make a video of yourself at work with a family in your
    own agency to demonstrate some aspect of systemic
    practice. You need to prepare a 5 minute section to show to
    the group. This can be a negative or positive example and
    needs to be accompanied with a commentary about what
    you have learned about systemic practice from the example
    you are to show. You will need to negotiate to use a video
    in the agency, arrangements for borrowing equipment,
    confidentiality issues, etc.

2. Find someone in your work context who would be
    prepared to act as a consultant to your thinking and practise
    with a family or organisational dilemma. This could entail
    live observation of you in practice plus one pre-session
    consultation meeting, live session consultation and one
    post-session consultation. This might involve careful work
    for the course participant to negotiate access to an
    appropriate person through their line management. The
    person could be their line manager, colleagues or others.
    Other key members of the agency could be invited to attend
    the consultation.

3. What connections do you make between your position in your own family and your work as a family therapist? Draw a geneogram and write a paragraph in response to this.

4. Write up three consecutive sessions with the same family in your agency (provide format), indicating:

    (a) the feedback from the family during and after each session;

    (b) your response to this;

    (c) how you linked and used these should a student be in a predominantly management position, this task can be adapted to his/her attending three consecutive meetings/supervision session.

5. Develop some ideas on how to get support in your agency for systemic work. The group can be divided into geographical sub-groups or groups of their choice to work on this, beginning with the suggestion that members of the sub-groups should share their professional geneograms with each other.

Chapter 10

"WHAT CAN YOU DO WHEN...?"
FIRST AID FOR
STUCK TEACHERS

Chapter 10

"What can you do when...?"
First Aid for Stuck Teachers

INTRODUCTION

In this section we present some of our ideas on how to deal with tricky situations. Some of these situations arise at a time when it is possible to prepare one's response. For example, the situation where a group member consistently non-attends. Others happen *in situ* on the day and you have to deal with them on the spot. For example the video breaks down and a course member uses this as an opportunity to criticise the course. Reading this section may provide you with some ideas for coping with such situations. The principle behind our responses has been, wherever possible, to be able to appreciate these sticky situations as feedback about the learning of the group. When one cannot *not* respond with curiosity, the teacher's response needs to acknowledge the feedback in such a way as to continue to facilitate learning. Sometimes, however, we know we can only act so as to limit the potential damage to the teaching process.

1. A New Member Joins an Already Formed Group

In this situation, we have found it important not to have

the expectation that the new member will be able to participate in the group on equal terms with the other members. This denies the boundary between the new and old members. It also denies the new member's possible feelings of being excluded, de-skilled and not knowledgeable. We have prescribed that the new member should not join in with the group until they are ready to do so and suggested they take an observer role until that time. This allows the group and the new members to find their own level.

2. One Member Consistently Non-attends

This is a time when you run the risk of getting into an escalation with course participants. It is difficult not to see the non-attendance as negative feedback about your teaching and to get caught up in trying to persuade the member to attend by letter or phone. It is possible for the teacher to become quite punitive without being totally aware of it, for example, by not saving handouts for the missing member, not ensuring the person knows what preparation is needed for a subsequent session. We have found it important to remember that people have many things happening in their lives and that these sometimes spill over into their course time. People have different paces of learning and may have learned enough to digest for a while. On one occasion when this was happening, the teacher telephoned the group member in a holiday period to let her know she was missed, find out her reason for not attending (illness and preoccupation with her own past family patterns stirred up by the teaching), reassure her that she would be able to catch up and suggest she took the time she needed to rest and feel ready to return. She returned to the group the next session after the holiday.

3. One Person in the Group Learns More Quickly than Another

It is difficult to get the pace of teaching right and you will often get it wrong. A useful intervention for the teacher is to allow people to learn at their own pace. We have found it important to keep in mind people's different paces and rhythms of learning and that it is not possible for everyone in the group to own every idea that is presented. It is also important to read feedback carefully. When a person does not learn as much as you hope, it may not necessarily represent negative feedback about the teaching but feedback about the right amount for that person to take on at that time. It is important to keep engaged with that person and look for feedback that he or she is ready to move on. You could do this by making a point of saying something personal informally to each person in the group each session.

4. Visitors Ask if They Can Participate in a Session

This is a particularly difficult dilemma for a naive teacher who is not sure of the definition of the boundaries around the teaching. One's decision will need to be based on the stage of development of the group process. At the beginning, the boundary between the group and the outside world is not yet clearly defined and, to allow a visitor to enter and leave at this stage may define the boundaries so loosely that other people in the group may feel free to leave too. The effect on the teacher at this stage may be to de-skill one and challenge one's teaching authority. At a later stage, however, visitors can be quite helpful in offering feedback to the teacher and this is, in our view, the most useful position for a visitor and this needs to be clarified both with the visitor and the group beforehand. Most often visitors are not readily welcomed by the group or by the teacher because they are not seen to directly contribute to the teaching–learning-system and are therefore comfortably refused; however it is important to keep in mind the possibility of an interesting contribution at a certain stage in the development of the group; one that might prevent the experience becoming predictable, too comfortable or stale.

5. The Group Wants to Dwell on Issues

The dilemma for the trainer here is whether to respond to the feedback or continue with the course plan. We aim to find ways of addressing the group's preoccupation whilst achieving aims for the course; in this way we hope neither the group nor the teacher will feel cheated. An example of this was when a project was set up for the group members to write up three consecutive family therapy sessions. The group failed to give in their projects and the teacher initiated some discussion in the group for the reasons for this. The group became preoccupied with the difficulties of deciding how to record sessions. At this point, the teacher decided to spend some time that session on methods of recording family therapy sessions, rather than proceeding with all the planned programme for that session. This resulted in all group members being able to finish their projects. A counter example is the common one of role play going on too long. This can be useful even if it is not part of the teaching agenda; if the teacher allows this to happen, the teacher may however feel the experience had not been sufficiently useful and learning opportunities sacrificed and the group may ultimately feel this too.

6. The Teacher Gets Tired

When the teacher is not well, not feeling energetic or is not well enough prepared, we suggest a choice of exercises which ensures the group does most of the work, for example, a small group exercise, tape review or other activity from a store of "emergency provisions" (see under Sections 11 or 12 below).

This takes the teacher out of the action position and allows the group to behave in a different way which may facilitate their learning as well as allowing one a rest!

7. The Teacher Gets "Negative" Feedback

Some examples could be: "It is too rushed", "I feel like I don't know anything any more", "It doesn't apply to my work", "I don't see families", "The reading is too difficult". It is important to take this feedback seriously and deal with each issue. If you do not address these issues, they are likely to return and could escalate, risking damaging the learning in the group and the commitment of group members to the course. The teacher needs to have antennae operating for examples of this kind of feedback at all times and to acknowledge them in the group. Examples of possible responses are, for the complaint about difficult reading, to be careful about prescribing reading for a while until the group asks for it again – and then give an easy paper. For the complaint about things being too rushed, take time out for a general group discussion to find out which issues have not been addressed adequately or extend the time planned for the next exercise. Another way of dealing with feedback from individuals or small numbers of the group would be to meet with these individuals, pairs or small groups to explore their difficulties, for example about applying their ideas to their practice

8. Course Participants Ask for More

This is very exciting and rewarding for the teacher and the temptation is to give more and more. However, one needs to keep in mind the need to accommodate to requests as long as they do not breach the boundaries of the teaching relationship, leading to problems about defining the limits of the teaching learning system. For example, the group may ask to meet during holidays. The teacher does not need to be there and give an extra teaching session but may do what is necessary to facilitate the group to arrange a session for themselves, e.g., booking a room, lending tapes, etc.

9 There is an Odd Number of People for a Pairs Exercise

The options here are for the teacher to join the odd person or for the odd person to join another pair, making a three-some. The solution will be affected by the kind of exercise involved and the stage of the learning process. For example, if one was doing reframing in pairs, it would be acceptable to have a threesome or for the teacher to join the odd person. This would be less advisable at the beginning stages of a group as the teacher could have an inhibiting effect on the person working with him or her. If personal material was the subject of the exercise, again it might not be such a good idea for the teacher to work with one member as the effect might be to unbalance the group in terms of their connectedness with the teacher.

10. Someone in the Group Arrives Halfway through the Session

This potentially disturbs the work of the group as they and the late comer struggle with how to connect the new person with their work so far. The temptation may be to stop the group, explain the continuing process or to be punitive and treat their appearance as an interruption or intrusion; either affects the person's ability to connect with the group. We think it important to be welcoming and positive. The teacher could ask the person to join the group as an observer until they feel ready to join in. This seems to allow everyone to find their own level with the least disturbance to all.

11. **Course Participants do not Come or There is a Very Small Teaching Group (due to illness, transport difficulties, communication problems, etc.).**
    The problem here is that if you proceed with your plans for the session, most of the teaching group will have missed it and you will have the further problem of how to communicate what they have missed without boring the ones who attended. We have dealt with this by having a few ideas up our sleeves for such occasions. These are ideas which punctuate the session sequence allowing those who have attended to feel they are having something special, but continuing the general work of the group. For example:

    (a) A consultation for one or all of the group members on a case, using the other members of the group as consultation team.

    (b) Showing tape from previous work in the group for tape review.

    (c) Showing a teaching tape.

    (d) Forming an *ad hoc* family role play for interviewing practice.

    (e) An agency consultation for one or all of the group members, using the other members of the group as consultant team.

    (f) Discussion of reading.

It seems important for the continuity of the course that part of the planned agenda should take place to ensure that those who attend see the session as connected to the course and not merely a holding meeting.

12. **The teacher is ill or absent**
    Again the problem is of depriving the group of continuity. If it is known about in advance, however, it can allow the group the opportunity to plan something for themselves or

for the teacher to plan something for the group to do by themselves and challenges the notion that course members need a teacher there to learn. For example:

(a)   The group can be asked to plan a session for themselves (some examples above and rely on the group's creativity to come up with others, some of which may give valuable feedback about their current preoccupations).

(b)   The group can be asked to have a reading session, catching up on course reading.

(c)   The group can be set homework or projects (see Chapter 5).

It is possible to build this eventuality into the group by asking them to have a plan should this occur during the course.

13. The Equipment Fails

It can be extremely difficult if you have planned a session which depends on the use of equipment and it fails to work, e.g., showing a tape, videotaping a session, use of a sound system. However, it is important not to get thrown by this as it happens many times in"real life" in people's agencies, so it is as well to think beforehand about how to cope when it happens.

(a)   Again, it is possible to fall back on an "up the sleeve" session as given under Section 11. above.

(b)   Alternatively, you can still do some sessions without equipment, asking people to take transcripts in place of video taping as this is a valuable exercise in itself and allows a discussion of this process and how to do it effectively.

(c)   Without a sound system, it is still possible for a team to observe non-verbal behaviour and offer the therapist their thoughts on this. Again this is an interesting exercise in itself and challenges the therapist to behave in a different way both with the family and with the team.

14. Course Participants Fail to do Necessary Reading or Homework for the Session

The problem here is that some members of the group will have done the necessary work and, if you abandon the session or change it too much to accommodate for the members who have not done it, you will disqualify both yourself as a teacher and the course members who have done the work.

(a)   In a session when we asked people to prepare a review of a current family therapy article, we asked people who had not done it to imagine they had written an article themselves and to describe the main themes and the journal to which they would submit it and the expected response.

(b)   Members of the group can be grouped to present the results of their reading and those who have not done it can be given the task of interviewing the others to find out the main points. This serves the purpose of provoking their activity in a session where otherwise they might take a passive role and also helps the people who have read to clarify their thinking.

(c)   When some people handed in written work and others did not despite reminders, we wrote written feedback to each of the people who had done it and gave it to them in sealed envelopes with some ceremony. The idea was to give individual attention to those who had done the work and provoke curiosity in those who had not done it to receive their own input.

(d)   We offered individual tutorial sessions to those who had done specific projects to share feedback and it was made clear to those who completed the work that this would also be offered to them when their projects came in.

15. Key Members of the Group do not Attend

This is a problem if the people in the group who were asked to prepare a case or reading material fail to attend. It runs the risk of scuppering the session.

(a) Again, some of the suggestions given under Section 14 above apply here.

(b) If someone to present a case had failed to turn up, some of the suggestions under Section 11 above also apply.

(c) Use of an *ad hoc* family around a specific issue, e.g., child sexual abuse, mental health problems, etc.; can be valuable as a focus for skills work and offers the additional advantages of avoiding some of the emotional involvement which sometimes gets in the way of using a real case for mainly skills work; people tend to feel less responsible for the outcome of the case and therefore freed to take a few therapeutic risks.

CONCLUSION

We hope this book will be used as a handbook by teachers of family therapy. As a resource for teachers, the book contains some of our experience in learning to teach effectively in the context of the part-time Introductory and Intermediate courses described in Chapter 1. Not only will the reader have ideas of what to do but also some ideas of what *not* to do. Having a repertoire for what *not* to do is as important in being an effective teacher as having a well packaged course. This is because successful and effective teaching, like successful and effective therapy, depends largely on the teacher's ability to first observe and then use feedback. Inability or failure to observe and use feedback within the teaching–learning system will lead to a disconnectedness between teacher and course participants. Once this begins, and if it goes unnoticed, the process of sharing and exchanging ideas and questions and being influenced by new information is interrupted and possibilities for learning and change rapidly diminish We need to emphasise this is as much a problem for teachers as course participants.

Because of our emphasis on the use of feedback we hope the reader will have become excited by the opportunities presented by the different kinds of response from course participants to our exercises.The book also attempts to show that, in creating a triangular relationship in the classroom of teacher, course participant and course participant's agency, the resources for teaching and learning are greatly increased. In our teaching we pay a lot of attention to the way the ideas we offer are more or less useful to course participants in their agencies and work settings. We invite course participants to tell and show us what works and what does not work as they carry out their professional roles and tasks as agents of change with families and other systems.

The exercises and homework described in the book demonstrate how we try to help course participants to adapt systems thinking and practice to their agencies. We spend a lot of time looking with course participants at how they can understand the feedback in their agency and from their colleagues. As they become interested and curious about the effect they are having on their work setting they move to an observer position that facilitates learning and impacts their agency system. Our present recruiting patterns show more than one person coming from the same agency for the same course as well as colleagues of 1989 course participants applying for the 1990 course.

We have much more teaching material than we have included in the book and can offer readers more examples of exercises, tasks, reading lists, syllabi. We also invite you, the reader, to give us feedback that will be useful as we plan further syllabi and teaching.

Please write to us at either: Karnac Books,

or at

The Tavistock Clinic,
120 Belsize Lane,
London NW3 5BA.

References

Andersen, T. (1984) 'The Reflecting Team: Dialogue and Meta-dialogue in Clinical Work.' *Family Process.*

Anderson, H., Goolishian, H. and Windermand, L. (1987) 'Problem determined systems: towards transformation in family therapy.' *Journal of Strategic and Systemic Therapies,* 5, 4, pp. 1–13.

Barot, R. (1988) 'Social anthropology, ethnicity and family therapy.' *Journal of Family Therapy,* 10, pp. 271–282.

Bateson, G. (1973) 'The cybernetics of "self": a theory of alco-holism,' in *Steps to an Ecology of Mind.* Paladin: London, pp. 280–308.

Bennun, I. (1986) 'Evaluating family therapy: a comparison of the Milan and problem solving approaches.' *Journal of Family Therapy,* 8, 3, pp. 235–242.

Burnham, J. (1986) *Family Therapy, First Steps Towards a Systemic Approach.* Tavistock: London.

Campbell, D., Reder, P., Draper, R. and Pollard, D. (1983) *Working with the Milan Method: Twenty Questions.* Occasional Paper, Institute of Family Therapy: London.

Campbell, D., Draper, R. and Huffington, C. (1988) *Teaching*

Systemic Thinking. Karnac: London.

Campbell, D., Draper, R. and Huffington, C. (1989) *Second Thoughts on the Theory and Practice of the Milan Approach to Family Therapy.* Karnac: London.

Campbell, D. and Draper, R., Eds (1985) *Applications of Systemic Family Therapy: the Milan Approach.* Grune and Stratton: London.

Cecchin, G. (1988) 'Hypothesizing, circularity, and neutrality revisited: an invitation to curiosity.' *Family Process,* **26,** pp. 405–413.

Fisch, R. *et al.* (1982) *The Tactics of Change: Doing Therapy Briefly.* Jossey-Bass: San Francisco.

Fleuridas, C. *et al.* (1986) 'The evolution of circular questioning – training family therapists.' *Journal of Marital and Family Therapy,* **12,** pp. 113–127.

Goldner, V. (1988) 'Generation and gender: normative and covert hierarchies.' *Family Process,* **27,** pp. 17–31.

Gorell Barnes, G. (1984) *Working with Families.* McMillan Education: London.

Gorell Barnes, G. and Campbell, D. (1982) 'The impact of structural and strategic approaches on the supervision process: A supervisor is supervised.' In Whiffen, R. and Byng-Hall, J. (Eds) *Family Therapy Supervision: Recent Developments in Practice.* Academic Press: London.

Haley, J. (1980) *Leaving Home.* McGraw Hill: New York.

Israelstam, K. (1988) 'Contrasting four major family therapy paradigms.' *Journal of Family Therapy,* **10,** pp. 179–196.

Lau, A. (1984) 'Transcultural issues in family therapy.' *Journal of Family Therapy,* **6,** pp. 91–112.

Liddle, H. A. (1982) 'On the problem of eclecticism; A call for epistemologic clarification and human-scale theories.' *Family Process,* **21,** pp. 243–250.

Lindsey, C. (1985) Consultation with professional and family systems in the context of residential and fostering services: In and out of care. In Campbell, D. and Draper, R. (Eds) *Applications of Systemic Family Therapy: The Milan Approach.* Grune and Stratton: London.

Madanes, C. (1981) *Strategic Family Therapy*. Jossey-Bass: San Francisco.

Maturana, H. (1978) 'Biology of language: the epistemology of reality.' In Miller, G.A. and Lennenberg, E. (Eds), *Psychology and Biology of Language and Thought*. Academic Press: New York.

Maturana, H. (1988) 'Reality: The search for objectivity or the quest for a compelling argument.' *Irish Journal of Psychology*, **9**, 1, pp. 25–82.

Maturana, H. and Varela, F. (1980) *Autopoiesis and Cognition: the Realization of the Living*. Reidel: Boston.

McGoldrick, M., Pearce, J. K. and Giordano, J., Eds (1982) *Ethnicity and Family Therapy*. Guilford Press: New York.

Minuchin, S. (1974) *Families and Family Therapy*. Tavistock: London.

Minuchin, S. and Fishman, C. (1981) *Family Therapy Techniques*. Harvard University Press: Cambridge, Mass.

Papp, P. (1983 *The Process of Change*. Guilford Press: New York.

Penn, P. (1982) 'Circular questioning.' *Family Process*, **21**, 3, pp. 267–280.

Penn, P. (1985) 'Feed-forward: future questions, future maps.' *Family Process*, **24**, 3, pp. 299–310.

Robinson, M., *et al.* (1985) 'A family systems approach to conciliation and separation in divorce.' *Journal of Family Therapy*, **7**, 4. pp. 357–378.

Satir, V. (1972) *People Making*. Science and Behaviour Books: Palo Alto.

Selvini Palazzoli, M. (1980) 'Why a long interval between sessions.' In Andolfi, M. and Zwerling, I. (Eds), *Dimensions of Family Therapy*. Guilford Press: New York.

Selvini Palazzoli, M., Boscolo, L., Cecchin, G. and Prata, G. (1978) *Paradox and Counterparadox*. Aronson: New York.

Selvini Palazzoli, M., Boscolo, L., Cecchin, G. and Prata, G. (1980) 'The problem of the referring person.' *Journal of Marital and Family Therapy*, **6**, 1, pp. 3–9.

Selvini Palazzoli, M., Boscolo, L., Cecchin, G. and Prata, G. (1980) 'Hypothesizing – circularity – neutrality: three guidelines for the conductor of the session.' *Family Process*, **19**, 1, pp. 3–12.

Sluzki, C. and Ransom, D., Eds, (1976) *Double Bind: The*

Foundation of the Communicational Approach to the Family. Grune and Stratton: New York.

Stanton, M. D. and Todd, T. C. (1981) 'Engaging "resistant" families in treatment.' *Family Process,* 20, pp. 261–293.

Tomm, K. (1984a) 'One perspective on the Milan systemic approach: Part I. Overview of development, theory and practice.' *Journal of Marital and Family Therapy,* 10, 2, pp. 113–125.

Tomm, K. (1984b) 'One perspective on the Milan systemic approach: Part II. Description of session format, interviewing style and interventions.' *Journal of Marital and Family Therapy,* 10, 3, pp. 253–271.

Tomm, K. (1987) 'Interventive interviewing: Part I. Strategizing as a fourth guideline for the therapist.' *Family Process,* 26, pp. 3–13.

Tomm, K. (1987) 'Interventive interviewing: Part II. Reflexive questioning as a means to enable self healing.' *Family Process,* 26, pp. 167–183.

Tomm, K. (1987) 'Interventive interviewing: Part III.' *Family Process,* 27, pp. 1–15.

Von Foerster, H. (1981) *Observing Systems.* Seaside: California.

Von Glasenfeld, E. (1984) 'An introduction to radical constructivism.' In Watzlawick, P. (Ed.), *The Invented Reality.* W.W. Norton: New York.

Walters, M. *et al.* (1988) *The Invisible Web: Gender Patterns in Family Relations.* Guilford Press: New York.

Whiffen, R. and Byng-Hall, J., Eds (1982) *Family Therapy Supervision.* Grune and Stratton: London.

Appendix 1

Reading Lists: Part I

1988/1989 – FAMILY THERAPY PART I

Books – General

Barnes, G. Gorell (1984) *Working with Families*. Macmillan: London.

Burnham, J. B. (1986) *Family Therapy. First Steps Towards a Systemic Approach*. Tavistock: London.

Haley, J. (1987) *Problem-Solving Therapy*. 2nd edition. Jossey-Bass: London. (First published 1976).

Hoffman, L. (1981) *Foundations of Family Therapy: A Conceptual Framework for Systems Change*. Basic Books: New York.

Morawetz, A. and Walker, G. (1984) *Brief Family Therapy with Single-parent Families*. Brunner/Mazel: New York. *Chapter 2* – The theoretical perspective: a systems approach, pp. 29–41.

Minuchin, S. (1974)   *Families and Family Therapy.* Tavistock: London.

Papp, P., Ed., (1977)   *Family Therapy: Full Length Case Studies.* Gardner Press: New York.

Treacher, A. and Carpenter, J., Eds, (1984) *Using Family Therapy. A Guide for Practitioners in Different Professional Settings.* Basil Blackwell: Oxford.

Articles

Aponte, H. (1984)   The negotiation of values in therapy. *Family Process*, **24**, 328–338.

Byng-Hall, J. (1979)   Re-editing family mythology during family therapy. *Journal of Family Therapy*, **1**, 103–116.

Carpenter, J. and Treacher, A. (1983) On the neglected but related arts of convening and engaging families and their wider systems. *Journal of Family Therapy*, **5**, 337–358.

Carter, B. and McGoldrick, M. (1980) The family life cycle and family therapy: an overview. In Carter, B. and McGoldrick, M. *The Family Life Cycle: A Framework for Family Therapy.* Gardner Press: New York, 3–20.

Kingston, P. (1982)   Power and influence in the environment of family therapy. *Journal of Family Therapy*, **4**, 211–227.

Kraemer, S. (1983)   Why I am not a family therapist. *Changes*, **2**, 1, 8–10.

Lau, A. (1984)   Transcultural issues in family therapy. *Journal of Family Therapy*, **6**, 91–112.

Teismann, M. W. (1980) Convening strategies in family therapy. *Family Process*, **19**, 393–400.

1988/1989 – FAMILY THERAPY PART I

Books – Systemic

Boscolo, L., Cecchin, G., Hoffman, L. and Penn, P. (1987) *Milan Systemic Family Therapy*. Basic Books: New York.

Campbell, D. *et al.* (1983) *Working with the Milan Method: Twenty Questions*. Institute of Family Therapy: London.

Campbell, D. and Draper, R. (1985) *Applications of Systemic Therapy: The Milan Approach*. Grune and Stratton for IFT: London.

Palazzoli, M. S. *et al.* (1978) *Paradox and Counterparadox*. Aronson: New York.

Articles

Bateson, G. (1973) The cybernetics of self. A theory of alcoholism. In *Steps to an Ecology of Mind*. Paladin: St Albans, pp. 280–308.

Cade, B. (1980) Strategic Therapy. *Journal of Family Therapy*, **2**, 89–99.

Cade, B. (1979) The use of paradox in therapy. In Walrond-Skinner, S. (Ed.) *Family and Marital Psychotherapy*. R & KP: London, pp. 91–105.

Fleuridas, C. *et al.* (1986) The evolution of circular questioning – training family therapist. *Journal of Marital and Family Therapy*, **12**, 113–127.

Jenkins, H. (1980) Paradox: a pivotal point in therapy. *Journal of Family Therapy*, **2**, 339–350.

Madanes, C. (1980) Protection, paradox and pretending. *Family Process*, **19**, 73–85.

Madanes, C. (1980)   Marital therapy when a symptom is presented by a spouse. *International Journal of Family Therapy*, 2, 120–121.

MacKinnon, L. (1983) Contrasting Strategic and Milan therapies. *Family Process*, 22, 425–441.

Morawetz, A. and Walker, G. (1984) The initial interview as a microcosm of therapy. In *Brief Family Therapy with Single-parent Families*. Brunner/Mazel: New York.

O'Brian, C. and Bruggen, P. (1985) Our personal and professional lives: learning positive connotation and circular questioning. *Family Process*, 24, 311–322.

Palazzoli, M. S. (1977) Family rituals. A powerful tool in family therapy. *Family Process*, 16, 445–453.

Palazzoli, M. S. (1980) Why a long interval between sessions. In Andolfi, M. and Zwerling, I. (Eds) *Dimensions of Family Therapy*. Guilford Press: New York, pp. 161–170.

Palazzoli, M. S. (1984) Behind the scenes of the organization: some guidelines for the expert in human relations. *Journal of Family Therapy*, 6, 299–307.

Palazzoli, M. S. (1985) The emergence of a comprehensive systems approach. Supervisor and team problems in a district psychiatric centre. *Journal of Family Therapy*, 7, 135–146.

Palazzoli, M. S. *et al.* (1978) A ritualised prescription in family therapy: odd days and even days. *Journal of Marriage and Family Counselling*, 4, 3, 3–9.

Palazzoli, M. S. *et al.* (1980) Hypothesizing–circularity–neutrality: three guidelines for the conductor of the session. *Family Process*, 19, 3–12.

Penn, P. (1985)   Feed forward: future questions, future maps. *Family Process*, **24**, 299–310.

de Shazer, S. (1986)   Brief Therapy: focused solution development. *Family Process*, **25**, 207–222.

Simon, D. I. (1985)   Dr Boxford, a mythical consultant (a note on the use of the non-real resource). *Journal of Family Therapy*, **7**, 387–390.

Stanton, M. D. (1981) An integrated structural/strategic approach to family and marital therapy. *Journal of Marital and Family Therapy*, **7**, 427–439.

Tomm, K. (1984)   One perspective on the Milan systemic approach. Part I. *Journal of Marital and Family Therapy*, **10**, 113–125.

Tomm, K. (1984)   One perspective on the Milan systemic approach. Part II. *Journal of Marital and Family Therapy*, **10**, 253–271.

Watzlawick, P. and Coyne, J. C. (1980) Depression following stroke: brief, problem-focused family treatment. *Family Process*, **19**, 13–18.

Books – Strategic

Haley, J. (1987)   *Problem Solving Therapy*. Jossey-Bass: London

Haley, J. (1973)   *Uncommon Therapy: the Psychiatric technique of Milton Erickson*. W. W. Norton: New York.

Watzlawick, P. *et al.* (1974) *Change: Principles of Problem Formation and Problem Resolution*. W. W. Norton: New York.

Articles:

Weakland, J. H. *et al.* (1974) Brief therapy: focused problem resolution. *Family Process*, **13**, 141–168.

1988/1989 – FAMILY THERAPY Part I

Supplementary Reading List to
Family Work with the Elderly

Bengtson, V. L. and Treas, J. (1980) The changing context of mental health and aging. In Birren, J. and Sloane, R. (Eds) *Handbook of Mental Health and Aging*. Prentice-Hall: Englewood Cliffs, NJ.

Blazer, D. & Siegler, I. C., Eds, (1984) *A Family Approach to Health Care of the Elderly*. Addison-Wesley: Menlo Park, Calif.

Brink, T. (1979)   Geriatric counselling: a practical guide. *Family Therapy*, **3**, 2, 163–168.

Brubaker, T., Ed. (1983) *Family Relationships in Later Life*. Sage: London.

Brubaker, T. (1983)   *Later Life Families*. Sage: London.

Clark, N. M. and Rakowski, W. (1983) Family caregivers of older adults: improving helping skills. *Gerontologist*, **23**, 637–642.

Cohen, M. (1982)   In the presence of your absence: the treatment of older families with a cancer patient. *Psychotherapy; Theory, Research and Practice*, **19**, 4, 453–460.

Corran,J. (1983)   Value of multi-generational counselling in objective client assessment. *Clinical Gerontologist*, **2**, 1, 61–62.

Duffy, M. (1984)   Aging and the family; intergenerational psychodynamics. *Psychotherapy*, **21**, 3, 342–346.

Eyde, D. R. and Rich, J. A. (1983) *Psychological Distress in Aging, A Family Management Model*. Aspen: Rockville, Md.

Gilewski, M., Kuppinger, J. and Zarit, S. (1985) The aging marital system: a case study in life changes and paradoxical intervention. *Clinical Gerontologist*, **3**, 3, 3–15.

Gilhooly, M. (1987)   Senile dementia and the family. In Orford, J. (Ed.) *Coping with Disorder in the Family.* Croom Helm: London.

Gilleard, C. J. (1984)   *Living with Dementia. Community Care of the Elderly Mentally Infirm.* Croom Helm: London.

Grauer, J., Betts, D. and Birnbom, F. (1973) Welfare emotions and family therapy in geriatrics. *Journal of the American Geriatrics Society*, **21**, 1, 21–24.

Gwyther, L. and Blazer, D. (1984) Family therapy and the dementia patient. *American Family Physician*, **29**, 5, 149–156.

Herr, J. and Weakland, J. (1979) *Counselling Elders and their Families.* Springer: New York.

Kilpatrick, A. (1968) Conjoint family therapy with geriatric patients. *Journal of the Fort Logan Mental Health Center*, **5**, 1, 29–35.

Kirschner, C. (1985)   Social work practice with the aged and their families: a systems approach. *Journal of Gerontological Social Work*, **8**, 4-3, 55–69.

LaWall, J. (1981)   Conjoint therapy of psychiatric problems in the elderly. *Journal of the American Geriatrics Society*, **29**, 2, 89–91.

Levin, E. *et al.* (1983) *The Supporters of Elderly Confused Persons at Home.* National Institute for Social Work, Mary Ward House, 5–7 Tavistock Place, London WC1H 9SS.

McEwan, E. (1987)   The whole grandfather: an intergenerational approach to family therapy. In

Sadavoy, J. and Leszcz, M. (Eds) *Treating the Elderly with Psychotherapy.* International Universities Press: Madison, Ct.

Pasnau, R., Fawzy, F. and Lansky, M. (1981) Organic Brain Syndrome and the Family. In Lansky, M. (Ed.) *Family Therapy and Major Psychopathology.* Grune and Stratton: New York.

Pinkstone, E. and Linsk, N. (1984) *Care of the Elderly; A Family Approach.* Pergamon: Oxford.

Pottle, S. (1984)   Developing a network-oriented service for elderly people and their carers. In Treacher, A. and Carpenter, J., Eds, (1984) *Using Family Therapy. A Guide for Practitioners in Different Professional Settings.* Basil Blackwell: Oxford.

Quinn, W. and Keller, J. (1981) A family therapy model for preserving independence in older people: utilisation of the family of procreation. *American Journal of Family Therapy,* **9,** 1, 79–84.

Ratna, L. and David, J. (1984) Family therapy with the elderly eentally ill: some strategies and techniques. *British Journal of Psychiatry,* **145,** 311–315.

Springer, D. and Brubaker, T. (1984) *Family Caregivers and Dependent Elderly, Minimizing Stress and Maximizing Independence.* Sage: London.

Walsh, F. (1980)   The family in later life. In Carter, E. and McGoldrick, M. (Eds) *The Family Life Cycle: A Framework for Family Therapy.* Gardner Press: New York.

Zarit, S. H. *et al.* (1985) *The Hidden Victims of Alzheimer's Disease. Families under Stress.* New York University Press: New York.

Statutory Work:

Dale, P. et al. (1986)   *Dangerous Families.* Tavistock: London.

Dimmock, B. and Dungworth, D. (1985) Beyond the family: using network meetings with statutory child care cases. *Journal of Family Therapy,* 7, 1.

Lindsey, C. (1985)   Consultations with professional and family systems in the context of residential and fostering services. In Campbell, D. and Draper, R. *Applications of Systemic Family Therapy.*

Little, M. and Conn, J. (1985) The application of systemic ideas and techniques to a child care system. In Campbell, D. and Draper, R. *Applications of Systemic Family Therapy.*

Reder, P. (1983)   Disorganized families and the helping professions: who's in charge of what? *Journal of Family Therapy,* 5, 1.

Reder, P. (1986)   Multi-agency family systems. *Journal of Family Therapy,* 8, 2.

Child Sexual Abuse:

Bentovim, A. (1987) Physical and sexual abuse of children; the role to the family therapist. *Journal of Family Therapy,* 9, 4.

Furniss, T. (1983)   Family process in the treatment of inter-familial child sexual abuse. *Journal of Family Therapy,* 5, 263–278.

Furniss, T. (1983)   Mutual Influence and Interlocking Professional-family process in the treatment of child sexual abuse and incest. *Child Abuse and Neglect,* 7, 207–223.

Community Mental Health:

Paraminteny *et al.*   Systemic family work within a community mental health centre by a community psychiatric nursing team. In Campbell, D. and Draper, R. *Applications of Systemic Family Therapy.*

Fruggeri *et al.*   The systemic approach in a mental health service. In Campbell, D. and Draper, R. *Applications of Systemic Family Therapy.*

Psychiatric In-Patient Work:

Berkowitz, R. (1984)   Therapeutic intervention with schizophrenic patients and their families. *Journal of Family Therapy*, 6, 3.

Jones, E. (1987)   Brief systemic work in psychiatric settings when a family member has been diagnosed as schizophrenic. *Journal of Family Therapy*, 9, 1.

Nitzberg *et al.*   In-patient hospital systemic consultation. In Campbell, D. and Draper, R. *Applications of Systemic Family Therapy.*

Pearlmutter *et al.* (1987) On not recommending family therapy to families in psychiatric emergency. *Family Systems Medicine*, 5, 3.

Working with Families with a Dying Member:

Acworth, A. and Bruggen, B. (1985) Family therapy when one member is on the death bed. *Journal of Family Therapy*, 7, 4.

Black, D. (1984)   Mourning and the Family. In Walrond-Skinner (Ed.) *Developments in Family Therapy.*

Black, D. and Lieberman, S. Loss, mourning and grief. In Bentovim *et al.* (Eds) *Family Therapy:*

Complementary Frameworks of Theory and Practice.

Conciliation/Stepfamilies:

L'Abate, L. (1981) Skills training programme for couples, families. In Gurman and Kniskern (Eds) *Handbook of Family Therapy.*

Robinson, M. and Parkinson, L. (1985) A family systems approach to conciliation in separation and divorce. *Journal of Family Therapy, 7, 4.*

Visher E.B. and Visher J.S. (1985) Stepfamilies are different. *Journal of Family Therapy, 7, 1, 9–18.*

1989/1990 – A SYSTEMS APPROACH TO FAMILIES AND ORGANISATIONS – Part I

Articles:
1. O'Brien, C. and Bruggen, P. (1985) Our personal and professional lives: learning positive connotation and circular questioning. *Family Process, 24, 311–322.*

2. Palazzoli, M. S. *et al.* (1980) The problem of the referring person. *Journal of Marital and Family Therapy, 6, 3–9.*

3. Haley, J. (1975) Why a mental health clinic should avoid family therapy. *Journal of Marriage and Family Counselling, 1, 3–13.*

4. Cecchin, G. (1987) Hypothesizing, circularity and neutrality revisited: an invitation to curiosity. *Family Process, 26, 405–413.*

5. Weakland, J. H. *et al.* (1974) Brief therapy: focused problem resolution. *Family Process, 13, 141–168.*

6. Ugazio, V. (1985) Hypothesis making: the Milan approach revisited. In Campbell, D. and Draper, R. (Eds) *Applications of Systemic Family Therapy. The Milan Approach.* Grune and Stratton: London, pp.23–32.

7. Tomm, K. (1987) Interventive interviewing: Part II. Reflexive questioning as a means to enable self-healing. *Family Process*, 26, 167–183.

8. Fleuridas, C. *et al.* (1986) The evolution of circular questions: training family therapists. *Journal of Marital and Family Therapy*, 12, 113–127.

9. Palazzoli, M. S. *et al.* (1980) A ritualised prescription in family therapy: odd days and even days. *Journal of Marital and Family Therapy*, 6, 3–9.

10. Rohrbaugh, M. *et al.* (1981) Compliance, defiance and therapeutic paradox: guidelines for strategic use of paradoxical interventions. *American Journal of Orthopsychiatry*, 51, 454–467.

11. Lau, A. (1984) Transcultural issues in family therapy. *Journal of Family Therapy*, 6, 91–112.

12. Goldner, V. (1988) Gender and generation. Normative and covert hierarchies. *Family Process*, 27, 17–31.

13. Hare-Mustin, R. T. (1987) The problem of gender in family therapy theory. *Family Process*, 26, 15–27.

14. Palazzoli, M. S. (1985) The emergence of a comprehensive systems approach: supervisor and team problems in a district psychiatric centre. *Journal of Family Therapy*, 7, 135–146.

15. Woodruff, A. F. and Engle, T. (1985) Strategic therapy and agency development: using circular thinking to turn the corner. *Journal of Strategic and Systemic Thinking*, 4, 4, 25–29.

16. Blount, A. (1985) Changing realities in the firm. *Journal of Strategic and Systemic Thinking*, **4**, 4, 40–52.

17. De Shazer, S. and Molnar, A. (1984) Changing teams/ changing families. *Family Process*, **23**, 481–486.

18. De Shazer, S. (1984) The death of resistance. *Family Process*, **23**, 11–17.

Books:

1. Campbell, D. *et al.* (1989) *Second Thoughts on the Theory and Practice of the Milan Approach to Family Therapy.* DC Associates: London.

2. Burnham, J. B. (1986) *Family Therapy.* Tavistock: London.

3. Palazzoli, M. S. *et al.* (1978) *Paradox and Counterparadox.* Aronson: New York.

4. Boscolo, L. *et al.* (1987) *Milan Systemic Family Therapy.* Basic Books: New York.

5. Hoffman, L. (1981) *Foundations of Family Therapy: a Conceptual Framework for Systems Change.* Basic Books: New York.

6. Haley, J. (1987) *Problem-Solving Therapy.* 2nd Ed., Jossey-Bass: London (First published 1976).

   Haley, J. (1973) *Uncommon Therapy.* W. W. Norton: New York.

7. Madanes, C. (1984) *Behind the One Way Mirror.* Jossey-Bass: Washington, London.

8. Watzlawick, P. *et al.* (1974) *Change: Principles of Problem Formation and Problem Resolution.* W. W. Norton: New York.

9. Minuchin, S. (1974) *Families and Family Therapy.* Tavistock: London.

10. Minuchin, S. and Fishman, H. C. (1982) *Family Therapy Techniques.* Harvard University Press: Cambridge, Mass.

11. Bateson, G. (1973) *Steps to an Ecology of Mind.* Paladin: St Albans. The cybernetics of 'self': a theory of alcoholism. pp. 280–308.

12. Palazzoli, M. S. *et al.* (1986) *The Hidden Games of Organisations.* Pantheon Books: New York.

13. Wynne, L. *et al.,* Eds, (1986) *Systems Consultation. A New Perspective for Family Therapy.* Guilford Press: New York.

Additional reading list:

1. Haley, J. (1973)   *Uncommon Therapy.* W. W. Norton: New York. (Chapter 2 – The family life cycle, pp. 41–64.)

2. Palazzoli, M. S. *et al.* (1980) Hypothesizing – circularity – neutrality: three guidelines for the conductor of the session. *Family Process,* **19,** 3–12.

3. Penn, P. (1982)   Circular questioning. *Family Process,* **21,** 267–280.

4. Aponte, H. (1985) The negotiation of values in therapy. *Family Therapy,* **24,** 323–328.

5. Campbell, D. *et al.* (1983) *Working with the Milan Method: Twenty Questions.* Institute of Family Therapy: London.

6. Barot, R. (1988)   Social anthropology, ethnicity and family therapy. *Journal of Family Therapy,* **10,** 271–282.

7   McGoldrick, M. *et al.,* Eds, (1982) *Ethnicity and Family Therapy.* Guilford Press: New York.

8. MacKinnon, L. (1983) Contrasting strategic and Milan therapies. *Family Process*, 22, 425–435.

9. MacKinnon, L. *et al.* (1984) Strategies of family therapy, the relationships, the styles of family functioning. *Journal of Strategic and Systemic Therapies*, 3, 6–22.

10. Papp, P. (1980)   The Greek chorus and other techniques of paradoxical therapy. *Family Process*, 19, 45–57.

11. Andersen, T. (1987) The reflecting team – dialogue and meta-dialogue in clinical work. *Family Process*, 26, 415–448.

12. Checkland, P. (1981) *Systems Thinking, Systems Practice*. Wiley: Chichester.

also the following:

1. Miller, R. and Bor, R. (1988) *AIDS: a Guide to Clinical Counselling*. Science Press: London.

2. Carter, E. and McGoldrick, M. *et al.*, Eds, (1989) *The Changing Family Life Cycle: a Framework for Family Therapy*. 2nd Ed. Allyn and Bacon: London.

3. Special Issue of   *Journal of Strategic and Systemic Therapies*, 1985, 4, 4.

4. Dell, P. (1989)   Violence and the systemic view: the problem of power, *Family Process*, 28, 1–14.

5. Hodes, M. (1989) Annotation: culture and family therapy. *Journal of Family Therapy*, 11, 117–128.

6. Cox, J. L., Ed. (1986) *Transcultural Psychiatry*. Croom Helm: London. (Chapter by R. Littlewood.)

7. McGoldrick, M. and Rohrbaugh, M. (1987), Researching ethnic family stereotypes. *Family Process*, 26, 89–99.

8. McGoldrick, M. *et al.*, Eds (1982) *Ethnicity and Family Therapy.*
    Guilford Press: New York.

9. Falicov, C. J., Ed. (1983) *Cultural Perspectives in Family Therapy.*
    Aspen: Rockville, Md. (Chapter by
    J. Lappin.)

Circular Questioning:

Burnham, J. (1986)   *Family   Therapy.*   Tavistock: London.
                       (Chapter 7 – Interviewing I, pp. 108–123.)

Fleuridas, C. (1986)   The evolution of circular questions: training
                       family therapists. *Journal of Marital and
                       Family Therapy*, **12**, 113–127.

Palazzoli, M. S. *et al.* (1980) Hypothesizing – circularity –
                       neutrality: three guidelines for the
                       conductor of the session. *Family Process*, **19**,
                       3–12.

Penn, P. (1982)   Circular questioning. *Family Process*, **20**,
                       267–280.

Penn, P. (1985)   Feed forward: future questions, future maps.
                       Family Process, **24**, 299–310.

Tomm, K. (1987)   Interventive interviewing: Part II. Reflexive
                       questioning as a means to enable self-
                       healing. *Family Process*, **26**, 167–183.

Tomm, K. (1988)   Interventive interviewing: Part III. Intend-
                       ing to ask lineal, circular, strategic and
                       reflexive questions. *Family Process*, **27**, 1–15.

**1990/1991 – A SYSTEMS APPROACH TO FAMILIES
AND ORGANISATIONS – Part I**

Books:

Burnham, J. B. (1986) *Family   Therapy.   First   Steps   Towards   a
                       Systemic Approach.* Tavistock: London.

Checkland, P. (1981)   *Systems Thinking, Systems Practice.* Wiley: Chichester.

Hoffman, L. (1981)   *Foundations of Family Therapy: A Conceptual Framework for Systems Change.* Basic Books: New York.

Keeney, B. P. (1983)   *Aesthetics of Change.* Guilford Press: New York.

Keeney, B. P. and Ross, J. M. (1985)*Mind in Therapy. Constructing Systemic Family Therapies.* Basic Books: New York.

Kotter, J. P. (1982)   *The General Managers.* Collier Macmillan: London.

Kotter, J. P. and Lawrence, P. R. (1974) *Mayors in Action: Five Approaches to Urban Governance.* Sage: London.

Morgan, G. (1986)   *Images of Organisation.* Sage: London.

Schein, E. H. (1985)   *Organisational Culture and Leadership: A Dynamic View.* Jossey-Bass: London.

Stewart, R. (1982)   *Choices for the Manager: Guide to Managerial Work and Behaviour.* McGraw-Hill: London.

Articles Summer Term 1991:

Boscolo, L. *et al.* (1987) *Milan Systemic Family Therapy.* Basic Books: New York.

Chiesa, M. (1986)   The Milan systemic approach to family therapy: an overview. *Free Associations,* **5,** 28–47.

Israelstam, K. (1988) Contrasting four major family therapy paradigms: implications for family therapy training. *Journal of Family Therapy,* **10,** 179–196.

McKinnon, L. (1983) Contrasting strategic and Milan therapies. *Family Process*, 22, 425–440.

Palazzoli, M. S. *et al.* First session of a systemic family therapy. *Unpublished paper.*

Palazzoli, M. S. *et al.* (1980) Hypothesizing – circularity – neutrality: three guidelines for the conductor of the session. *Family Process*, 19, 3–12.

Palazzoli, M. S. *et al.* (1978) *Paradox and Counterparadox*. Aronson: London.

Penn, P. (1982)   Circular questioning. *Family Process*, 20, 267–280.

Penn, P. (1985)   Feed forward: future questions, future maps. *Family Process*, 24, 299–310.

Tomm, K. (1984)   One perspective on the Milan Systemic Approach: Part I. Overview of development, theory and practice. *Journal of Marital and Family Therapy*, 10, 113–125.

Tomm, K. (1984)   One perspective on the Milan Systemic Approach: Part II. Description of session format and interviewing style and intervention. *Journal of Marital and Family Therapy*, 10, 253–271.

Tomm, K. (1987)   Interventive interviewing: Part I. Strategising as a fourth guideline for the therapist. *Family Process*, 26, 3–13.

Tomm, K. (1987)   Interventive interviewing: Part II. Reflexive questioning as a means to enable self-healing. *Family Process*, 26, 167–183.

Tomm, K. (1988)   Interventive interviewing: Part III. Intending to ask lineal, circular, strategic and reflexive questions. *Family Process*, 27, 1–15.

Reading Lists: Part II

1988/1989 – FAMILY THERAPY – Part II

Books:

Bateson, G. (1973)   *Steps to an Ecology of Mind*. Paladin: St Albans.

Boscolo, I. *et al.* (1987) *Milan Systemic Family Therapy*. Basic Books: New York.

Burnham, J. (1986)   *Family Therapy*. Tavistock: London.

Campbell, D. and Draper, R., Eds (1985) *Applications of Systemic Therapy: The Milan Approach*. Grune and Stratton: London.

De Shazer, S. (1985)   *Keys to Solution in Brief Therapy*. W. W. Norton: London.

De Shazer, S. (1982)   *Patterns of Brief Family Therapy*. Guilford Press: New York.

Falicov, C. J. (1983)   *Cultural Perspectives in Family Therapy.*
Aspen: Rockville, Md.

Hoffman, L. (1981)   *Foundations of Family Therapy: a Conceptual
Framework for Systems Change.* Basic Books:
New York.

Keeney, B. P. and Ross, J. M. (1985) *Mind in Therapy. Constructing
Systemic Family Therapies.* Basic Books:
New York.

Keeney, B. P. and Silverstein, O. (1986) *The Therapeutic Voice of
Olga Silverstein.* Guilford Press: New York.

Madanes, C. (1981)   *Strategic Family Therapy.* Jossey-Bass: San
Francisco.

Morawetz, A. and Walker, G. (1981) *Brief Therapy with Single-
parent Families.* Brunner/Mazel: New York.

Papp, P. (1983)   *The Process of Change.* Guilford Press: New
York.

Zilbach, J. J. (1986)   *Young Children in Family Therapy.* Brunner/
Mazel: New York.

Articles:

Byng-Hall. J. (1980)   Symptom bearer as marital distance
regulator: clinical implications. *Family
Process,* **19,** 355–365.

Byng-Hall, J. (1982)   The use of the earphone in supervision. In
Whiffen, R. and Byng-Hall, J. (Eds) *Family
Therapy Supervision.* Academic Press:
London, pp. 47–56.

Cecchin, G. (1987)   Hypothesizing, circularity and neutrality
revisited: an invitation to curiosity. *Family
Process,* **26,** 405–413.

De Shazer, S. *et al.* (1986) Brief therapy: focussed solution
development. *Family Process,* **25,** 207–222.

Elkaim, M. (1986)   A systemic approach to couple therapy. *Family Process*, **25**, 35–42.

Goldner, V. (1985)   Feminism and family therapy. *Family Process*, **24**, 31–47.

Goldner, V. (1988)   Gender and generation. Normative and covert hierarchies. *Family Process*, **27**, 17–31.

Hoffman, L. (1985)   Beyond power and control: toward a second order family systems theory. *Family Systems Medicine*, **3**, 381–396.

Liddle, H. A. (1985)   Five factors of failure in structural–strategic family therapy: a contextual construction. In Coleman, S. B. (Ed.) *Failures in Family Therapy*. Guilford Press: New York, pp. 152–189.

Madanes, C. (1980)   Protection, paradox and pretending. *Family Process*, **19**, 73–85.

Palazzoli, M. S. (1985) The problem of the sibling as the referring person. *Journal of Marital and Family Therapy*, **11**, 21–34.

Papp, P. (1980)   The Greek chorus and other techniques of paradoxical therapy. *Family Process*, **19**, 45–57.

Pilalis, J. and Anderton, J. (1986) Feminism and family therapy – a possible meeting point. *Journal of Family Therapy*, **8**, 99–114.

Plone, A. (In Press)   Marital and existential pain: dialectic in Bergman's "Scenes from a Marriage". *Family Process*.

Sheinberg, M. (1985) The debate: a strategic technique. *Family Process*, **24**, 259–271.

Tomm, K. (1987)   Interventive interviewing: Part II. Reflexive questioning as a means to enable self-healing. *Family Process*, 26, 167–183.

Tomm, K. (1988)   Interventive interviewing: Part III. Intending to ask lineal, circular, strategic and reflexive questions. *Family Process, 27,* 1–15.

1990/1991 – A SYSTEMS APPROACH TO FAMILIES AND ORGANISATIONS – Part II

Autumn Term 1990:

Aponte, H. (1985)   The negotiation of values in therapy. *Family Process*, 24, 323–328.

Boyd-Franklin, N. (1989) *Black Families in Therapy. A Multisystems Approach.* Guilford Press: New York.

Burnham, J. B. (1986) *Family Therapy. First Steps Towards a Systemic Approach.* Tavistock: London.

Campbell, D. *et al.* (1989) *Second Thoughts on the Theory and Practice of the Milan Approach to Family Therapy.* DC Associates: London.

Carter, B. (1989)   Gender-sensitive therapy. *Family Therapy Networker*, 13, 4, 57–60.

Cecchin, G. (1987)   Hypothesizing, circularity and neutrality revisited: an invitation to curiosity. *Family Process*, 26, 405–413.

Dell, P. (1989)   Violence and the system view: the problem of power. *Family Process*, 29, 1–14.

Fleuridas, C. *et al.* (1986) The evolution of circular questions: training family therapists. *Journal of Marital and Family Therapy*, 12, 113–127.

Goldner, V. (1988)   Gender and generation. Normative and covert hierarchies. *Family Process*, 27, 17–31.

Gurman, A. S. and Kniskern, D. P., Eds (1981) *Handbook of Family Therapy*. Brunner/Mazel: New York.

Haley, J. (1987)   *Problem-solving Therapy.* 2nd Ed., Jossey-Bass: London (First published 1976).

Haley, J. (1973)   *Uncommon Therapy.* W. W. Norton: New York.

Hare-Mustin, R. T. (1987) The problem of gender in family therapy theory. *Family Process*, **26**, 15–27.

Hoffman, L. (1981)   *Foundations of Family Therapy: a Conceptual Framework for Systems Change.* Basic Books: New York.

Jones, E. (1988)   The Milan method – Quo Vadis? *Journal of Family Therapy*, **10**, 325–338.

Lappin, J. (1983)   On becoming a culturally conscious family therapist. In Falicov, C. J., Ed. (1983) *Cultural Perspectives in Family Therapy.* Aspen: Rockville, Md.

McGoldrick, M. and Rohrbaugh, M. (1987), Researching ethnic family stereotypes. *Family Process*, **26**, 89–99.

McKinnon, L. (1983) Contrasting strategic and Milan therapies. *Family Process*, **22**, 425–440.

Madanes, C. (1987)   *Behind the One Way Mirror.* Jossey-Bass: London.

Penn, P. (1982)   Circular questioning. *Family Process*, **20**, 267–280.

Penn, P. (1985)   Feed forward: future questions, future maps. *Family Process*, **24**, 299–310.

Pilalis, J. and Anderton, J. (1986) Feminism and family therapy – a possible meeting point. *Journal of Family Therapy*, **8**, 99–114.

Palazzoli, M. S. *et al.* (1980) A ritualised prescription in family therapy: odd days and even days. *Journal of Marital and Family Therapy*, 6, 3–9.

Papp, P. (1980)   The Greek chorus and other techniques of paradoxical therapy. *Family Process*, 19, 45–57.

Rohrbaugh, M. *et al.* (1981) Compliance, defiance and therapeutic paradox: guidelines for strategic use of paradoxical interventions. *American Journal of Orthopsychiatry*, 51, 454–467.

Skynner, A. C. R. (1976) *One Flesh: Separate Persons. Principles of Family and Marital Psychotherapy.* Constable: London.

Skynner, A. C. R. and Cleese, J. (1983) *Families and How to Survive Them.* Methuen: London.

Tomm, K. (1987)   Interventive interviewing: Part I. Strategising as a fourth guideline for the therapist. *Family Process*, 26, 3–13.

Tomm, K. (1987)   Interventive interviewing: Part II. Reflexive questioning as a means to enable self-healing. *Family Process*, 26, 167–183.

Tomm, K. (1988)   Interventive interviewing: Part III. Intending to ask lineal, circular, strategic and reflexive questions. *Family Process*, 27, 1–15.

Ugazio, V. (1985)   Hypothesis making: the Milan approach revisited. In Campbell, D. and Draper, R., Eds (1985) *Applications of Systemic Therapy: The Milan Approach.* Grune and Stratton: London.

Walters, M. *et al.* (1988) *The Invisible Web: Gender Patterns in Family Relations.* Guilford Press: New York.

Watzlawick, P. *et al.* (1974) *Change. Principles of Problem Formation and Problem Resolution.* W. W. Norton: New York.

Watzlawick, P. *et al.* (1967) *Pragmatics of Human Communications.* W. W. Norton: New York.

Weakland, J. H. *et al.* (1974) Brief therapy – focused problem resolution. *Family Process,* **13,** 141–168.

Spring Term 1991:
1.   *Models of Change and Causation – Bateson, Dell and Maturana*

Andersen, T. (1987)   The reflecting team – dialogue and meta-dialogue in clinical work. *Family Process,* **26,** 415–428.

Anderson, H. and Goolishian, H. (1986) Problem determined systems – towards transformation in family therapy. *Journal of Strategic and Systemic Therapies,* **5,** 1–13.

Bateson, G. (1973)   *Steps to an Ecology of Mind.* Paladin: St Albans. (Towards a theory of schizophrenia, pp. 173–198; The logical categories of learning and communication, pp. 250–279; The cybernetics of "self" a theory of alcoholism, pp. 280–308.)

Cade, B. (1980)   Strategic Therapy. *Journal of Family Therapy,* **2,** 89–99.

Campbell, D. and Draper, R., Eds (1985) *Applications of Systemic Therapy: The Milan Approach.* Grune and Stratton: London.

Cronen, V. E. *et al.* (1985) A dialectic view of personal change. In Davis, K. E. and Gergen, K. J. (Eds) *The Social Construction of the Person.* Springer Verlag: New York, pp. 203–224.

Davidson, J. *et al.* (1988) The reflecting team. *Family Therapy Networker,* **12,** 5, 44–46, 76–77.

De Shazer, S. *et al.* (1986) Brief therapy: focused solution development. *Family Process*, **25**, 207–221.

De Shazer, S. (1988)   Constructing solutions. *Family Therapy Networker*, **12**, 5, 42–43.

Dell, P. F. (1985)   Understanding Bateson and Maturana: towards a biological foundation for the social sciences. *Journal of Marital and Family Therapy*, **11**, 1–20.

Dimmock, B. and Dungworth, D. (1983) Creating manoeuverability for family systems therapists in social services departments. *Journal of Family Therapy*, **5**, 53–69.

Glaser, D. and Frosh, S. (1988) *Child Sexual Abuse*. British Association for Social Workers: London.

Golann, S. (1988)   On second-order family therapy. *Family Process*, **27**, 51–65.

Journal of Strategic and Systemic Therapies (1985) Special Issue, **4**, 4.

MacKinnon, L. *et al.* (1984) Strategies of family therapy: the relationship to styles of family functioning. *Journal of Strategic and Systemic Therapies*, **3**, 3, 6–22.

Mason, B. (1989)   *Handing Over. Developing Consistency Across Shifts in Residential and Health Settings*. DC Publishing: London. (Chapter 1 – The problem of traditional handover, pp. 9–12; Chapter 2 – The systemic handover, pp. 13–18; Chapter 3 – Some theoretical considerations, pp. 19–28; Chapter 4 – Some ideas which have influenced the development of the systemic handover, pp. 29–33.)

Mendez, C. L. *et al.* (1988) The bringing forth of pathology. *Irish Journal of Psychology*, **9**, 1, Special Issue, 144–172.

Miller, R. and Bor, R. (1988) *AIDS: a Guide to Clinical Counselling*. Science Press: London.

Minuchin, S. and Fishman, H. C. (1981) *Family Therapy Techniques*. Harvard   University   Press: London. (Chapter 7 – Enactment, pp. 78–97.)

Palazzoli, M. S. *et al*. (1989) *Family Games. General Models of Psychotic Processes in the Family*. Karnac Books: London.

Palazzoli, M. S. *et al*. (1978) *Paradox and Counterparadox*. Aronson: New York.

Simon, R. (1988)   Like a friendly editor. An interview with Lynn Hoffman. *Family Therapy Networker*, **12**, 5, 55–58, 74–75.

Tomm, K. and Lannamann, J. (1988) Questions as Interventions. *Family Therapy Networker*, **12**, 5, 38–41.

Summer Term 1991:

For Discussion
Andersen, T. (1987)   The reflecting team – dialogue and meta-dialogue in clinical work. *Family Process*, **26**, 415–428.

Bateson, G. (1973)   *Steps to an Ecology of Mind*. Paladin: St Albans. (The cybernetics of 'self' a theory of alcoholism, pp. 280–308.)

Hoffman, L. (1990)   Constructing realities: an art of lenses. *Family Process*, **29**, 1.

Additional References:
Aderman, J. and Russell, T. (1990) A constructivist approach to working with abusive and neglectful parents. *Family Systems Medicine*, **8**, 241–250.

Boscolo, L. *et al*. (1987) *Milan Systemic Family Therapy*. Basic Books: New York. (Introduction, pp. 3–28.)

Boyd-Franklin, N. (1989) *Black Families in Therapy. A Multi-Systems Approach.* Guilford Press: New York. (Chapters 6 and 8.)

Burnham, J. B. (1986) *Family Therapy. First Steps Towards a Systemic Approach.* Tavistock: London. (Chapter on 'Failure'.)

Dell, P. F. (1985)   Understanding Bateson and Maturana: towards a biological foundation for the social sciences. *Journal of Marital and Family Therapy,* 11, 1–20.

Leyland, M. L. (1988) An introduction to some of the ideas of Humberto Maturana. *Journal of Family Therapy,* 10, 357–374.

McGoldrick, M. (1982) Ethnicity and family therapy: an overview. In McGoldrick, M. *et al.* (Eds) *Ethnicity and Family Therapy.* Guilford Press: New York, pp. 3–30.

Walters, M. *et al.* (1988) *The Invisible Web: Gender Patterns in Family Relations.* Guilford Press: New York.

Reading Lists: Part III

1989/1990 – SYSTEMIC PRACTICE IN THE WORK SETTING – Part III

Andersen, T. (1987)   The reflecting team – dialogue and meta-dialogue in clinical work. *Family Process*, **26**, 415–448.

Bott, D. and Hodes, M. (1989) Structural therapy for a West African family. *Journal of Family Therapy*, **11**, 169–179.

Byng-Hall, J. (1982)   The use of the earphone in supervision. In Whiffen, R. and Byng-Hall, J. (Eds) *Family Therapy Supervision*. Academic Press: London, pp. 47–56.

Davidson, J. *et al.* (1988) The reflecting team. *Family Therapy Networker*, **12**, 5, 44–46, 76–77.

Fleuridas, C. *et al.* (1986) The evolution of circular questions:

training family therapists. *Journal of Marital and Family Therapy*, **12**, 113–127.

Goldner, V. (1988)   Generation and gender. Normative and covert hierarchies. *Family Process*, **27**, 17–31.

Hodes, M. (1989)   Annotation: culture and family therapy. *Journal of Family Therapy*, **11**, 117–128.

Journal of Strategic and Systemic Therapies (1989) Special bonus issue: Family Therapy with immigrant families. **8**, Summer, 40pp.

Kassis, J. P. (1984)   A team's development from universe to multiverse. *Journal of Strategic and Systemic Therapies*, **3**, 4, 63–72.

Kinnon, U. (1988)   Racism Awareness – who helps the client? *Journal of Social Work Practice*, **3**, 3, 80–92.

Libow, J. A. (1985)   Gender and sex role issues as family secrets. *Journal of Strategic and Systemic Therapies*, **4**, 32–41.

McGoldrick, M. *et al.*, Eds (1982) *Ethnicity and Family Therapy*. Guilford Press: New York. (See especially Chapters 1, 4, 5, 6, 10 & 26.)

Roberts, M. *et al.* (1989) Reflecting team consultations. *Journal of Strategic and Systemic Therapies*, **8**, 2 & 3, 38–46.

Tomm, K. (1987)   Interventive interviewing: Part I. Strategising as a fourth guideline for the therapist. *Family Process*, **26**, 3–13.

Tomm, K. (1987)   Interventive interviewing: Part II. Reflexive questioning as a means to enable self-healing. *Family Process*, **26**, 167–183.

Tomm, K. (1988)   Interventive interviewing: Part III. Intending to ask lineal, circular, strategic and reflexive questions. *Family Process*, **27**, 1–15.

1990/1991 – SYSTEMIC PRACTICE IN THE WORK SETTING – Part III

Andersen, T. (1987) The reflecting team: dialogue and meta-dialogue in clinical work. *Family Process*, **26**, 415–428.

Boyd-Franklin, N. (1989) *Black Families in Therapy. A Multi-Systems Approach*. Guilford Press: New York.

Burns, R. C. and Kaufman, S. H. (1972) *Actions, Styles and Symbols in Kinetic Family Drawings*. Butterworths: London.

Davidson, J. *et al.* (1988) The reflecting team. *Family Therapy Networker*, **12**, 5, 44–46, 76–77.

Furniss, T. (1983) Mutual influence and interlocking profess-ional-family process in the treatment of CSA and incest. *Child Abuse and Neglect*, **7**, 207–223.

Goldner, V. (1988) Generation and gender. Normative and covert hierarchies. *Family Process*, **27**, 17–31.

Lindsey, C. Consultations with professional and family systems in the context of residential and fostering services. In Campbell, D. and Draper, R. (Eds) *Applications of Systemic Family Therapy: The Milan Approach*. Grune and Stratton: London, pp. 221–227.

MacKinnon, L. and Miller, D. (1987) The new Epistemology and the Milan Method: feminist and sociopolitical considerations. *Journal of Marital and Family Therapy*, **13**, 139–155.

McGoldrick, M. *et al.*, Eds (1982) *Ethnicity and Family Therapy.*
    Guilford Press: New York.

Messent, P.   Making links. Working with Bangladeshi
                     families in the East End. IFT Unpublished
                     Dissertation.

O'Brian, C. (1990)   Family therapy with black families. *Journal
                     of Family Therapy,* 12, 3–16.

Perelberg, R. and Miller, A. (1990) *Gender and Power in Families.*
    Routledge: London.

Reder, P. (1986)   Multi-agency family systems. *Journal of
                     Family Therapy,* 8, 139–152.

Sluzki, C. (1979)   Migration and family conflict. *Family
                     Process,* 18, 379–390.

Weakland, J. and Jordan, L. Child protective services: when you
    have to work briefly with reluctant clients.

Webb-Woodard, L. and Woodard, B. (1983) The larger system in
    the treatment of incest. *Journal of Strategic
    and Systemic Therapies,* 2, 3, 28–37.

Wilkinson, S. (1985) Drawing up boundaries: a technique.
                     Journal of Family Therapy, 7, 99–112.

1990/1991 – SYSTEMIC PRACTICE
IN THE WORK SETTING – Part III

Anderson, H. and Goolishian, H. (1988) A view of human
    systems as linguistic systems: some prelim-
    inary ideas about the implications for
    clinical theory. *Family Process,* 27, 371–393.

Bateson, G. (1973)   *Steps to an Ecology of Mind.* Paladin: St
                     Albans. (The cybernetics of 'self' a theory
                     of alcoholism, pp. 280–308. See also
                     Psychiatry, 1971, 34, 1–18.)

Bateson, G. (1973)   Double bind: towards a theory of schizophrenia. In *Steps to an Ecology of Mind*. St Albans: Paladin, pp. 242–249.

Burnham, J. B. (1986) *Family Therapy. First Steps Towards a Systemic Approach*. Tavistock: London.

Dell, P. (1986)   In defence of linear causality. *Family Process*, 25, 513–521.

Erickson, G. (1988)   Against the grain: decentering family therapy. *Journal of Marital and Family Therapy*, 14, 225–236.

Goldner, V. (1985)   Feminism and family therapy. *Family Process*, 24, 31–47.

Haldane, D. and McCluskey, U. (1982) Existentialism and family therapy: a neglected perspective. *Association for Family Therapy Newsletter*, 1982.

Jackson, D. D. (1957) The question of family homeostasis. *Psychiatric Quarterly Supplement*, 31, 79–90.

Kempler, W. (1981)   *Experiential Psychotherapy Within Families*. Brunner/Mazel: New York.

Koestler, A. (1967)   *The Ghost in the Machine*. Hutchinson: London.

Laing, R. D. (1970)   *Knots*. Tavistock: London. (Reprinted by Penguin: London, 1972.)

Maturana, H. *et al.* (1988) The bringing forth of pathology. *Irish Journal of Psychology*, 9, 1, Special Issue, 144–172.

Minuchin, S. and Fishman, H. C. (1981) *Family Therapy Techniques*. Harvard University Press: Cambridge, Ma.

Minuchin, S. (1989)   My voices: an historical perspective.

Journal of Family Therapy, Special Issue, 69–80.

Napier, A. Y. and Whitaker, C. A. (1978) *The Family Crucible*. Harper & Row: London.

Pascal, B. (1970)   *Pensées*. Penguin Classics: Harmondsworth. (Originally published, 1906.)

Penn, P. (1985)   Feed forward: future questions, future maps. *Family Process*, **24**, 299–310.

Van Deurzen-Smith, E. (1984) Existential therapy. In Dryden, W. (Ed.) *Individual Therapy in Britain*. Harper & Row: London, pp. 149–174.

Walrond-Skinner, S. and Watson, D., Eds (1987) *Ethical Issues in Family Therapy*. Routledge & Kegan Paul: London.

Whitaker, C. A. and Keith, D. V. (1981) Symbolic-experiential family therapy. In Gurman, A. and Kniskern, D. (Eds) *The Handbook of Family Therapy*. Brunner/Mazel: New York.

Whitaker, C. A. (1990) *Midnight Musings of a Family Therapist*. W. W. Norton: New York.

1990/1991 – SYSTEMIC PRACTICE IN THE WORK SETTING – Part III

Adult Children of Alcoholics, ACOA, (1990) Self-help or self-pity? Series of articles. *Family Therapy Networker*, **14**, 1, Jan-Feb, 22–43.

Aderman, J. and Russell, T. (1990) A constructivist approach to working with abusive and neglectful parents. *Family Systems Medicine*, **8**, 241–250.

Aldridge, D. (1988)   Treating self-mutilating behaviour: a social strategy. *Family Systems Medicine,*, **6**, 5–20.

Aldridge, D. and Rossiter, J. A. (1984) A strategic assessment of deliberate self harm. *Journal of Family Therapy*, **6**, 113–125.

Byng-Hall, J. (1980)   Symptom bearer as marital distance regulator: clinical implications. *Family Process*, **19**, 355–365.

Campbell, D. *et al.* (1989) *A Systemic Approach to Consultation*. DC Associates: London.

Coyne, J. C. (1984)   Strategic therapy with married depressed persons: initial agenda, themes and interventions. *Journal of Marital and Family Therapy*, **10**, 53–62.

Crowther, C. *et al.* (1990) "Why should we talk to you? You'll only tell the Court". On being an informer and a family therapist. *Journal of Marital and Family Therapy*, **12**, 105–122.

De Maio, R. (1989)   Integrating traditional alcoholic treatment programmes and family systems therapy. *Family Systems Medicine*, **7**, 274–291.

De Shazer, S. and Molnar, A. (1984) Four useful interventions in brief family therapy. *Journal of Marital and Family Therapy*, **10**, 297–304.

Dielman, C. *et al.* (1984) The strategic use of symptoms as metaphors in family therapy: some case illustrations. *Journal of Strategic and Systemic Therapies*, **3**, 2, 29–34.

Family Therapy Networker (1987) Families who battle the bottle. *Family Therapy Networker*, Special Issue, **11**, 4.

Goldner, V. (1988)   Generation and gender. Normative and covert hierarchies. *Family Process*, **27**, 17–31.

Hodes, M. (1989)   Annotation: culture and family therapy. *Journal of Family Therapy*, **11**, 117–128.

Kassis, J. P. (1984)   A team's development from universe to multi-verse. *Journal of Strategic and Systemic Therapies*, 3, 4, 63–72.

McGoldrick, M. *et al.*, Eds (1982) *Ethnicity and Family Therapy.* Guilford Press: New York. (See especially Chapters 1, 4, 5, 6, 10 & 26.)

Molnar, A. and De Shazer, S. (1987) Solution focused therapy: towards the identification of therapeutic tasks. *Journal of Marital and Family Therapy*, 13, 349–358.

Peaks, B. (1989)   Strategies for solving children's problems understood as behavioural metaphors. *Journal of Strategic and Systemic Therapies*, 8, 2 & 3, 226.

Swindell, L. (1988)   Group work with sexually abused young women. *F. S. U. Quarterly*, 43, 21–25.

Wynne, L. C. *et al.* (1986) *Systems Consultation. A New Perspective for Family Therapy.* Guilford Press: New York.

Appendix 2

COURSE OUTLINES

1988/1989 – FAMILY THERAPY – Part I

Autumn Term

Week I: 7 October   Introduction and Expectations

Week II: 14 October   Observing Systemic Patterns

Week III: 21 October   Introduction to the Family Life Cycle

Week IV: 28 October   Hypothesising about Systems

Week V:
Week VI: 4 November   LONG DAY – Interviewing

Week VII: 11 November   The Wider Network
                              (guest teacher: Myrna Gower)

Week VIII: 18 November   Gender Issues in Systemic Work
                              (guest teacher: Charlotte Burke)

Week IX: 25 November   Student Presentations

Week X: 2 December   Student Presentations continued. Review of the Term, Projects for the Break

Spring Term

Week I: 13 January   Agency Context

Week II: 20 January   End-of-Session Interventions: Part I

Week III: 27 January   End-of-Session Interventions: Part II

Week IV: 3 February   The Interview as an Intervention: Part I

Week V: 10 February

Week VI: LONG DAY – The Interview as an Intervention: Part II

Week VII: 17 February   Cross-Cultural Issues in Working with Families

Week VIII: 24 February   Theories of Change: Part I (guest teacher: Myrna Gower)

Week IX: 3 March   Theories of Change: Part II

Week X: 10 March   Family Therapy Map Project

Summer Term

Week I: 28 April   Family Therapists and Their Families

Week II: 5 May   Structural and Strategic/Systemic Styles: Learning to Work Differently

Week III: 12 May   Building on Skills (using the one-way screen)

Week IV: 19 May   Reframing & Hypothesising
                                      Revisited

Week V: 26 May
Week VI: LONG DAY – Interviewing Skills

Week VII: 2 June   Agency Dilemmas
                                      (guest teacher: Charlotte Burke)

Week VIII: 9 June   The Team Behind the Screen

Week IX: 16 June   Schools of Family Therapy:
                                      A Debate

Week X: 23 June   Where to Next?

1989/1990 – FAMILY THERAPY – Part II:

Autumn Term

Week I: 7 October   Introduction

Week II: 14 October   The Dilemma of Change

Week III: 21 October   Debates and Split Messages

Week IV: 28 October   Half Term

Week V: 4 November   Joint Session. Gender and Family
                                      Therapy

Week VI: 11 November   Skills Development

Week VII: 18 November   Bateson's Ideas

Week VIII: 25 November   Milan Revisited

Week IX: 2 December   Devising Interventions

Week X: 9 December   Case Presentation

Spring Term

Week I:	13 January	Problems & Solutions, Strategic Therapy Revisited
Week II:	20 January	Further Adventures in Strategic Therapy
Week III:	27 January	Skills Development
Week IV:	3 February	Skills Development
Week V:	10 February	Strategic Therapy – Madanes
Week VI:	17 February	Ethnicity
Week VII:	24 February	Horses for Courses. Models, Contexts
Week VIII:	3 March	Back to Bateson
Week IX:	10 March	Back Home on the Ranch: Agency Issues

Summer Term

Week I:	21 April	Testing Hypotheses
Week II:	28 April	Circular Questioning
Week III:	5 May	Agency Issues
Week IV:	12 May	Use of Creativity and Humour Joint Session 10:00–3:00
Week V:	19 May	Skills Development & Tape Review
Week VI:	26 May	Couples Therapy
	2 June	Half Term – Possibility of Tape Viewing

Week VII: 9 June   Systemic Work with Individuals

Week VIII: 16 June   Dilemmas of Change:
                                The Reflecting Team

Week IX: 23 June   Feedback and Feedforward

**1989/1990 –A SYSTEMS APPROACH
TO FAMILIES AND ORGANISATIONS – Part II**

Autumn Term

Week I: 6 October   Consulting to Colleagues

Week II: 13 October   Back to Bateson

Week III: 20 October   The Dilemma of Change

Week IV: 27 October   The Use of Metaphor
                               (Guest: Peter Tapang)

Week V: 3 November   Feedback over Time

Week VI:
Week VII: 10 November   LONG DAY – Skills Profile

Week VIII: 17 November   Ethical Dilemmas

Week IX: 24 November   Expanding the Context of Systemic
                               Thinking

Week X: 1 December   Current Issues in Family Therapy

Reading List: Autumn Term

Week II: Bateson, G. (1972) Towards a theory of
                         schizophrenia. In *Steps to an Ecology of
                         Mind*. Paladin: London, pp. 173–198.

Week III: Watzlawick, P., Weakland, J. H. and

Fisch, R. (1974) *Change: Principles of Problem Formation and Problem Resolution.* W. W. Norton: New York. (Read two chapters of your choice.)

Week IV: To be Announced.

Week V: Walters, M., Carter, B., Papp, P. and Silverstein, O. (1988) *The Invisible Web: Gender Patterns in Family Relations.* Guilford Press: New York. (Read one case study of your choice.)

Week VI/VII: Carr, A. (1989) Chloe Madanes: comprehensive guide to strategic therapy. *Context* (Newsletter of AFT), 2, Summer, pp.11–14. (Plus re-read one of the skills papers from last year.)

Week VIII   Dell, P. F. (1989) Violence and the systemic view: the problem of power. *Family Process,* 28, 1–14.

Treacher, A. (1987) Family therapists are potentially damaging to families and their wider networks: Discuss. In Walrond-Skinner, S. and Watson, D. (Eds) *Ethical Issues in Family Therapy.* Routledge & Kegan Paul: London, pp. 87–103.

Week IX   (Read one paper from a current family therapy journal.)

Week X   Campbell, D. and Draper, R., Eds (1985) *Applications of Systemic Family Therapy.* Grune and Stratton: London. (Read Chapter 1, "Creating a context for change: An overview", and one chapter of your choice from each of Part II, "Teams", and Part III, "Agencies".)

Spring Term

Week I:	19 January	Expanding the Context of Systemic Thinking
Week II:	26 January	"Career Consultation" (Guest: Myrna Gower) and Related Agency Issues
Week III:	2 February	Curiosity, Neutrality and Changing Family Life Cycles – Part I
Week IV:	9 February	Curiosity, Neutrality and Changing Family Life Cycles – Part II
Week V:	16 February	Curiosity, Neutrality and Changing Family Life Cycles – Part III
Week VI:	23 February	LONG DAY – Neutrality in Interviewing
Week VII:		
2 March	**HALF TERM**	(Opportunity for work on projects)
Week VIII:	9 March	Systemic Thinking and Mental Health
Week IX:	16 March	Application of Systemic Thinking to Child Sexual Abuse (Guest: Sylvia Duncan)
Week X:	23 March	Working Systemically with Couples and Individuals

Reading List: Spring Term

Bentovim, A. (1988)   Implications from the Cleveland Report: a personal perspective. *Newsletter for AFT*, **8**, 4, Winter, 23–25.

Child, N. (1989)   Family Therapy: the rest of the picture.

Journal of Family Therapy, **11**, 281–296.

Campbell, D. (1985)   The consultation interview. In Campbell, D. and Draper, R. (Eds) *Application of Systemic Family Therapy.* Grune and Stratton: London.

Dimmock, B. and Dungworth, D. (1983) Creating manoeuvrability for family/systems therapists in social services departments. *Journal of Family Therapy*, **5**, 53–69.

Fleuridas, C. *et al.* (1986) The evolution of circular questioning – training family therapists. *Journal of Marital and Family Therapy*, **12**, 113–127.

Golann, S. (1988)   On second-order family therapy. *Family Process*, **27**, 51–65.

Haley, J. (1975)   Why a mental health clinic should avoid family therapy. *Journal of Marriage and Family Counselling*, 3–13.

Palazzoli, M.S. (1989) *Family Games: General Models of Psychotic Processes in the Family.* Karnac: London.

Walters, M., Carter, B., Papp, P. and Silverstein, O. (1988) Toward a feminist perspective in family therapy. In *The Invisible Web: Gender Patterns in Family Relations.* Guilford Press: New York, pp. 15–30.

Will, D. (1989)   Feminism, CSA, and the (long-overdue) demise of systems mystification. *Context*, **9**, 12–15.

Summer Term

Week I: 4 May   The Soaps: Opportunities for Script Writers (or "How to Use Your Training in Family Therapy")

Week II: 11 May   Setting Tasks

Week III: 18 May   Letters and Telephone Calls as
Interventions

Week IV: 25 May   Different Approaches to
Supervision

Week V: 1 June   Recording and Access: Techniques
and Ethics

Week VI:
8 June   LONG DAY – Video Presentations
Week VII: and Skills Practice

Week VIII: 15 June   Beginnings and Endings with
Families

Week IX: 22 June   Critique of Family Therapy Theory
and Practice

Week X: 29 June   "Discontinuous Leaps"

Reading List: Summer Term

Week I: (Just the "Soaps")

Week II: De Shazer, S. and Molnar, A. (1984) Four
useful interventions in brief family
therapy. *Journal of Marital and Family
Therapy,* **10.**

Week III: Wojcik J. V. and Iverson E. R. (1989)
Therapeutic letters: the power of the
printed word. *Journal of Strategic and
Systemic Therapy,* **8,** 77-81.

Week IV: Andersen, T. (1987) The reflecting team:
dialogue and meta-dialogue in clinical
work. *Family Process,* **26,** 415–428.

Andolfi, M. and Menghi, P. (1982)
Provocation supervision. In Whiffen, R.
and Byng-Hall, J. (Eds) *Family Therapy
Supervision.* Academic Press: London, pp.
181–196.

Breunlin, D. C. and Cade, B. (1981)
Intervening in family systems with
observer messages. *Journal of Marital and
Family Therapy,* 7, 453–460.

Heath, A. W. *et al.* Answering the call: a
manual for beginning supervisors. *Family
Therapy Networker,* 7, 36–37, 66.

Week V: Fonagy, P. *et al.* (1989) Evaluating the
                   performance of Departments of Psycho-
                   therapy. *Psychoanalytic Psychoherapy,* 4,
                   121–153.

Weeks VI & VII: Whiffen, R. (1982) The use of videotape in
                   Supervision. In Whiffen, R. and Byng-Hall,
                   J. (Eds) *Family Therapy Supervision.* London,
                   pp. 39–46.

Week VIII: Brockless, J. (1990) The effects of telephone
                   contact/prompting   on   subsequent
                   attendance at initial appointments at a
                   hospital Department of Child & Adoles-
                   cent Psychiatry. *Newsletter of the Association
                   for Child Psychology and Psychiatry,* 12, 5–8.

                   Jaffa, T. and Griffin, S. (1990) Does a
                   shorter wait for a first appointment
                   improve the attendance rate in child
                   psychiatry? *Newsletter of the Association for
                   Child Psychology and Psychiatry,* 12, 9–11.

                   Treacher, A. (1989) Termination in family
                   therapy: developing a structural approach.
                   Journal of Family Therapy, 11, 135–148.

Week IX:	Luepnitz, D. A. (1988) A feminist critique of eight approaches to family therapy. In *The Family Interpreted: Feminist Theory in Clinical Practice*. Basic Books: New York, pp. 30–105.
Week X:	(To be announced)

1988/1989 –A SYSTEMS APPROACH TO CHANGE IN FAMILIES AND ORGANISATIONS – Part I

Autumn Term

Week I:	Introduction to Change

Week II:	Systems – 1, 2, 3 persons
Week III:	Systems – Teams and Organisations

	plus	Different Points of View
		Hypothesizing
		Life and Developmental Cycles

Week IV:	Feedback

Week V:	The Meaning of Resistance to Change

Week VI:	Losses and Gains

Week VII:	Models of Change

Week VIII: Week IX:	The Process of Change

Week X:	Culture, Change and Meaning

1990–1991   SPRING TERM

Session I:	18 January	Culture Change & Meaning in Workers' Agency Context
Session II:	25 January	Resistance (Losses, Gains & Change)

Session III: 1 February   Resistance as Feedback

Session IV: 8 February   COURSE EVENT
with Students from Part II & Part III

Session V: 15 February   Models of Therapy and Skills

Session VI: 8 March   Models of Therapy Cases

Session VII: 15 March   Models/Cases
of Therapy continued

Session VIII: 22 March   Domains of Constraint:
Statutory Work
Children Act 1989
Review of Projects
& Learning

Summer Term

Session I: 26 April   Project Groups meet

Session II: 3 May   Overview of Term Consultation

Session III: 10 May   Rescheduled Course Event

Session IV: 17 May   Review Course Event Interviewing I

Session V: 24 May   Hypothesising and Interviewing II:
Intervening with your cases

HALF TERM PROJECT – 31 MAY

Session VI: 7 June   Positive Connotation

Session VII: 14 June   Interviewing III: Your cases

Session VIII: 21 June   Interviewing IV

Session IX: 28 June   Evaluation: The Art and Skill of
offering and receiving feedback

Session X: 5 July   Video Tape Review Project
Evaluation

Session XI: 12 July   Personal Change & Mental Maps –
Summer Project